The Healing Feeling

The Healing Feeling

RECIPES AND REMEDIES FROM AUSTRALIA'S
LEADING SPA CHEF

Samantha Gowing

THE HEALING FEELING

Disclaimer

The intention of this book is to offer a variety of integrative remedies and some culinary solutions to a healthier life. It is in no way a formal diagnosis, nor a dedicated cookbook.

Thanks to the Australian Traditional Medicine Society for this message.

The practice of natural medicine is holistic. The holistic practice of natural medicine also extends to the most appropriate modality, or type of therapy, both for the individual and the presenting health concerns. The properly trained natural medicine practitioner is well qualified to offer advice and guidance here. However it is often the person seeking better health who will first make this decision, based on their already known likes and dislikes, perhaps even their 'gut feeling'.

Third edition
First published in 2012
Copyright © Samantha Gowing 2012, 2013, 2014
Copyright photographs © individual photographers
ISBN 978-0-9875069-3-1

This edition published by Whole Happiness™ Publishing
Whole Happiness™ is a trademark of Gowings Restaurant Pty Ltd
PO Box 2208, Byron Bay, NSW, 2481, Australia.

All rights reserved. No part of this publication may be reproduced, stored in a retrieval system, or transmitted, in any form or by any means, electronic, mechanical, photocopying, digital transmission, recording or otherwise, without the prior permission of the publisher.

In loving memory of Dennis Gowing.

*To my students - past, present and future.
Each one should teach one.*

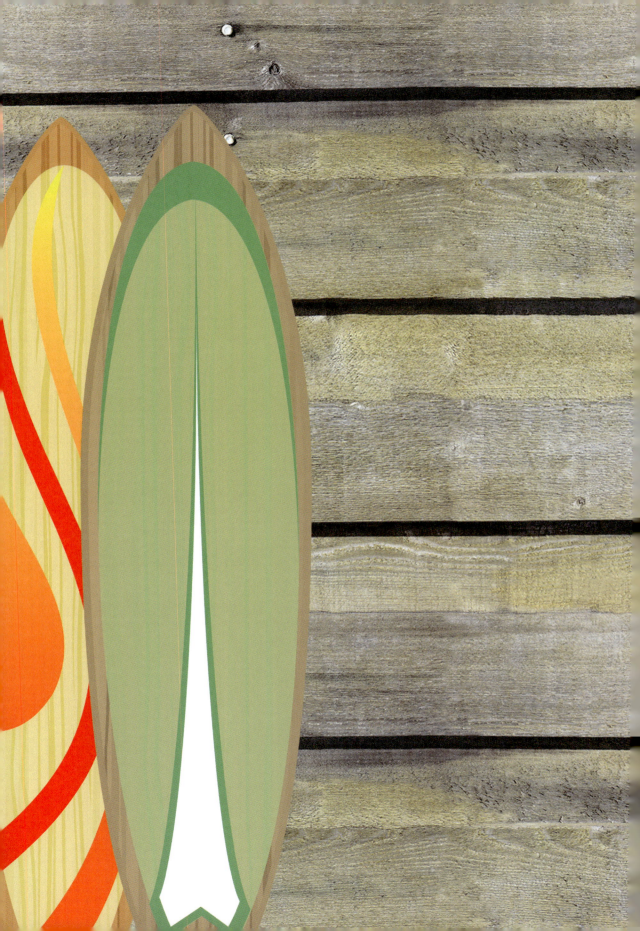

Ingredients

The Healing Feeling	14	Essential Enzymes	66
Byron Styling	17	The Gluten Solution	68
Surf Spa Food	19	Grain and Seed	72
Death of a Salesman	27	The Pulse of Life	89
Holy Tao!	29	Gland to Meet You	98
The Power of Food	31	Gland all Over	102
The Body In Balance	33	The Stinking Rose	106
Grill Seekers	35	The Jewels of the Underground	111
That Ol' Gut Feeling	37	Hustle, Bustle and Muscle	115
Beating those Underbelly Blues	39	A Vine Romance	118
Seasonality	42	Skin Deep	120
The Yeast Beast	54	Dedicated Coconut	125
Kelp is on its Way	57	Incas, Aztecs, Mayans & Mexicans	129
Miso Miscellany	58	Paleo Power	133
A Japanese fun guy	62	Grace and Gratitude	136

> "I had the good fortune of stumbling across Sam Gowing back in 2002, when she gave me a jolly-good dose of both Pilates and "food as medicine" advice.
>
> Since then, whenever I'm run down, flat out, over-roasted, or in need to some professional "energy support", she is the one I call.
>
> She always sets me back on the path to good health, and manages to do so in a way that makes food sexy, and exercise delightful.
>
> She has a big heart, and this makes her the real deal.
>
> I love her way."
>
> Clare Bowditch

Foreword

To me, Sam Gowing is just like the inspired and inspiring children's author Dr Seuss.

Theodor Seuss Geisel, who wrote over 60 children's books, is credited with some of the most fantastic and amusing stories, most of which had powerful but subtle messages about life. He was a true professional – allegedly spending 9 months to write what was to become his most iconic story - The Cat in the Hat, using a very limited vocabulary of only 250 different words.

He was succinct, irreverent, entertaining and enlightening, and made reading, a task that many children found un-enjoyable, a wonderful experience.

Sam Gowing is the Dr Seuss of health and nutrition. Sam has dedication and enthusiasm, knowledge and belief, which is second to none. She has a wonderful take on life, the way she explains things (and never down her nose at you) is clear and simple and I adore her sense of humour and word play.

At the age of 24 Sam became the licensee of the legendary Collingwood pub, the multi-award award winning Gowings Grace Darling Hotel. With her background in food for almost 30 years, and having sadly witnessed her beloved father Dennis' death from cancer, Sam re-trained as a clinical nutritionist.

Sam transplanted herself from the gritty inner Melbourne suburb of Collingwood to lush Byron Bay to further her holistic study, research and work. Oh, and surf.

Sam is an entrepreneur having created Food, Health, Wealth – which provides culinary and marketing solutions to the wellness industry. She mentors business people by coaching them to success, teaching them how to build an online presence and create strategic marketing campaigns just like her wise and witty Now and Zen e-newsletter - now in its tenth year - which contains recipes and ripper information.

She is in constant demand for corporate speaking engagements and cooking demonstrations and is a business mentor.

Sam is currently undertaking a new online postgraduate Master of Gastronomic Tourism (MGT) degree with world famous culinary arts and hospitality school, Le Cordon Bleu, in collaboration with Southern Cross University.

Quite simply Sam is a leader when it comes to her field.

This book, The Healing Feeling, contains vital information within its 30 chapters, which you will read again and again.

Sam has always been incredibly generous with the knowledge she has shared with friends and of course while working at Australia's leading health retreats and spas around the world and as founding Executive Chef and Nutritionist at the glorious Cabarita Ocean Health Retreat in New South Wales.

Here, however, everyone (like the kids Dr Seuss inspired) has the chance to read, be amused and enlightened by Sam.

She will inspire and empower you. I can vouch for that. So sit back, pour yourself a cup of chamomile tea and get ready for a fantastic adventure.

It was Dr Seuss who said, "Why try to fit in when you stand out?" and Sam is certainly one who stands out.

I am not sure if Sam will write 60 books, but this is certainly one brilliant book.

Flip Shelton
Muesli Maker, Mother
Rio de Janeiro

A *friendship across the seas*

It all began with yoga and the idea of a good health, well-being, yoga festival in Ubud. It transpired into a friendship across the seas that has spanned a decade of jokes and joyous meetings.

It has been said we are like sisters and there is no doubt that there is a timeless bond that unites us.

We share the same philosophy about eating and being supremely kind to ourselves, about only ever eating the finest food, savouring the finest wine and enjoying every minute of life.

Our medicine is love and laughter and, between the two of us, we are very good at that! Sam's knowledge about the secret life of food is extraordinary and I bow to her endless knowledge on all that is edible.

Janet DeNeefe
Founder & Director
Ubud Writers & Readers Festival
Bali

RECIPES AND REMEDIES FROM AUSTRALIA'S LEADING SPA CHEF

Samantha Gowing and Janet DeNeefe at the Maya, Ubud, Bali.

The Healing Feeling

My voyage across the nourishing waters toward the healing arts began when I was a teenager. I broke my leg riding my little green motor scooter on a crisp autumn Melbourne morning. I don't really remember how the accident happened, but clearly I was in the wrong place at the wrong time. Or was I? Everything happens for a reason and the memory of the impact is deliberately dim. I blacked out but then I saw the light.

My recollection of this is as clear now as it was the day it happened more than twenty-five years ago. I was floating and it felt as though I was being drawn to a higher, extraordinarily serene place that was light filled and calm. There was no struggle just clarity, an understanding and acceptance. I knew my physical body was on the ground and the body that carried me was part of that physical body but it also had a life of its own – effortless. As I was been drawn into the lighter place I had a sense that it was not the right time for me to leave my physical body – I hadn't said goodbye to anyone. I thought of my father and how much I would miss him.

As thoughts slowly gathered of my friends and family, I felt a shift in my energy and I began to descend from the place I had been. I felt myself move downwards and I became hyper aware of the force of gravity pulling at me. I could see my body sprawled on the ground and I had the sense of onlookers gathering around me then suddenly, with what seemed like a great thud, I was on the ground and filling out my physical body with the part that felt as though it had been floating. I slid into my body as if I was putting on an old pair of boots and all seemed ok, that is until I heard the siren of the ambulance and almost instantaneously I felt pain. Quickly I realised all was not well. I opened my eyes to see a posse of personal trainers from a nearby gym staring down at me. Naturally I thought I had died and gone to heaven until a paramedic peered through the crowd and then I knew it was kind of heaven on earth except this one hurt like hell.

The paramedics carted me off to the Alfred Hospital in Melbourne after asking me to wiggle my toes – phew – and I recall giggling all the way from South Melbourne with them.

When I was wheeled into casualty the attending nurse screamed at the sight of me and jeered away. Clearly things were still not good. She composed herself and returned swiftly and then I recognised her face – she was a girl I went to boarding school with and was probably in more shock than I was. Lucky for me I was able to whine and carry on a bit, begging for more of that surreal morphine that danced so gracefully through my entire being earlier. I was euphoric and felt blessed to have friends in high places. Or maybe that was just me in the 'high' place.

The next few days were a bit of a blur - intensive care has that effect – and it hurt a lot. I had patches of memory; immediate family, best friends around me and my father sobbing at my side, in his suit with his tie skewif - a sign he'd had too many drinks in

Seafood tasting platter.

his restaurant. Slowly I understood what had happened. I had snapped my right femur and managed a rather nasty compound fracture to my right tibia or shinbone. I'd also fractured my left radius and given my nose a good whack. Scars and bumps galore, I was lucky to be alive. I was nineteen.

Six weeks in traction at the Alfred hospital consisting of four-hourly intravenous pethidine administration accompanied by an anti-nausea shot. The "Jolly Lolly Trolley" as the wonderful nurses of Ward 4D called it would wheel in and whack me up. My tummy and bum bruised by the pin cushioning of those hideous needles. As weeks passed I found myself craving the needle more than the drug itself – go figure. Drug dependency in hospital is an interesting journey and so was astro-travelling around the ward at night.

You see, I was pinned to the bed in traction, held down by heavily weighted water bottles at the end of the bed to keep the broken bones of my right leg in one place so they could knit and heal. The fractures were so bad that I had a K-Rod inserted through the head of my femur diagonally down to the end of the shaft of my long bone. In addition, a plate with eight screws was inserted to hold the compound fracture of my tibia together which was so badly broken that the operating orthopedic surgeon had to laterally rotate my lower leg dramatically to one side so my bones could heal. This has left me with my right leg a few centimeters shorter – give or take the weather.

The pethidine doses diminished and soon I had two new friends I could depend on. I called them Vera Valium and Katie Codeine forte who dropped in every four hours. My mental state was somewhat synthetic and while the pain continued I was in a semi-state of acceptance and became quite accustomed to lying in bed all day watching TV and resting. As time passed I was encouraged to begin my long arduous road of physiotherapy. Yeoucharooni! My poor right leg had atrophied beyond recognition and worse still I could not move a muscle. I tried so hard to wiggle a toe and raise a foot but to no avail. Somehow during those frustrating final days in hospital I managed to get up and out of my horizontal home to be bathed and clumsily move from walking frame to crutches, stumbling like a disabled newborn calf.

Yoga found me about ten years after the injuries. In the beginning I could not even kneel. The scar tissue so entrenched that I had a limited range of motion. Back bends were a fantasy and seated twists nearly impossible. Slowly but surely I persisted with a practice, guided by a wonderful teacher in Fitzroy named Paul Wooden at his Gertrude Street Yoga centre. I soon joined the daily dawn classes and within a year I was amazed how my body responded to the movement and the breathing techniques. It is over fifteen years since I began my practice and I went onto teach yoga and Pilates for eight years. No student is too inflexible. Yoga is a journey and not a destination - and I am truly grateful for my connection to the sacred Sanskrit spiritual path.

Byron Styling

I'd had a gut full of the extreme Melbourne weather. Freezing and bleak in winter and the sweltering city heat in summer, so in 2008 I packed up my three legged dog Sly Bones and my best friend Nigel and we headed off for an unchartered adventure to Byron Bay where we have lived ever since. Well, Sly Bones has gone to the great organic kennel in the sky, but he spent his last year in paradise.

Byron is an awesome place to live because of the ocean, live entertainment and abundant produce of the Northern Rivers region. People are always asking where to go and what to do when you're here so here's some tips for you.

Byron Bay is famous for its hippy history and alternative surf culture. If you come to visit you must have a surfing lesson with Rusty Miller and practice yoga with either Byron Yoga Center or, for a more dedicated practitioner style of asana, try Ananta Yoga.

People are always asking where to go and what to do when you're here so here are some tips for you.

I recommend Targa on Marvel Street for the best breakfast in town and the real teapots that don't drip, and real tea leaves – the best green tea in town. Out of town a little is the fabulous Harvest Cafe in Newrybar. Not to be missed.

My weekly Paleo friendly survival meal are the great schnitzels and other treats at The Lazy Italian. A little place down Bay Lane, behind the Beach Hotel – just love it.

Fellow healthy foodie, friend and mentoring client Jemma Gawned's inspiring Naked Treaties is the bomb for sensational living green juices her superfood smoothies which I always have with a good pinch of E3Live. Also on Marvel Street.

We reckon all visitors buy ultra fresh fish from Freckle and his crew at the Byron Bay Seafood Market on Lawson Street. If you're here in winter, enjoy the whale migration.

Sunday through to Thursday is Happy Hour at the Byron at Byron Resort and Spa. Friday night at the Railway Friendly Bar (a.k.a. The Rails) is where you'll find the local community gathering for great food and free music nightly.

We have great entertainment here which was one of my main criteria for relocating. Local acts include Tijuana Cartel and an awesome singer called Lisa Hunt who sings about once a month on a Sundays at the Beach Hotel. Speaking of pubs, my punting life still thrives occasionally with a middy and a punt at The Great Northern.

Surf Spa Food

*"As I ate the oysters with their strong taste of the sea
and their faint metallic taste that the cold white wine washed away,
leaving only the sea taste and the succulent texture,
and as I drank their cold liquid from each shell
and washed it down with the crisp taste of the wine,
I lost the empty feeling and began to be happy and to make plans."*

Ernest Hemingway, A Moveable Feast

Not long after I moved to Byron Bay I stood up on a surfboard for the first time. Cashing in a birthday voucher, I was lucky enough to be guided by former US surfing pro Rusty Miller who gave me my wings. He taught me a kind of surf yoga on the beach – much to the delight of the locals – we danced like birds as he prepared me for my maiden voyage. Onshore I was encouraged to learn that the action of standing up was not dissimilar to that of Chataranga Dandasana, a yoga position that makes up part of the Vinyasa Flow.

Rusty shared some of his water knowledge with me, teaching me board safety, body balance, paddling techniques and restoring some of the ocean confidence I had lost when diving years before on the Great Barrier Reef. Delighted that I am a "goofy foot" – right leg leads – as my right leg is two and a half centimeter's shorter from the road accident mentioned earlier. After a few attempts of crawling and wiping out I managed to stand shakily for the first time – albeit not for long. When I finally stood up I hung on for dear life flapping my wings and focusing in the tip of the board as instructed. By the end of that initial lesson, I had clumsily surfed nearly a dozen waves and by the last two, the realisation dawned on me that it wasn't about controlling the board it was about moving and gliding along with the force of the wave prompting me to relax and let the energy of the wave move through me. I was hooked.

Surfing is a daily connection that becomes a part of your existence. It provides a deeper respect for the ocean and the Zen-like experience that it delivers when you are tuned into the immediate experience of what you are doing. Not before, not after, the right here and now. Laser focus, safety and skill combine with the negative ions of the water, the force and energy of the wave – a constant measure of energy, yet this is one we can measure and witness unlike those which are graphed.

Salad of Sea Vegetables with Kelp Noodles

Serves 4 as a side

1 packet kelp noodles.
Good handful of green leaves, washed and dried
1 toasted nori sheet, shredded
1 tablespoon arame seaweed, soaked and drained
1 tablespoon wakame seaweed, soaked and drained
2/3 cup activated almonds, roughly chopped
1 tablespoon pickled ginger, shredded

Dressing
1/3 cup macadamia nut oil
2 tablespoons mirin
1 tablespoon tamari
1 teaspoon white miso paste
Dash umeboshi plum vinegar
1 teaspoon grated ginger
1 lime, zest and juice

- Rinse and drain kelp noodles
- Combine sea vegetables, leaves and almonds
- Add pickled ginger
- Whisk dressing ingredients together well and blend into salad.

Living Cuisine

So here's the thing, I was never a fan of raw food – because of its cooling and abrasive effect on the digestive system for some – until I moved up to Byron Bay and then established the kitchen for a new health retreat. I started to investigate the merits of living foods and over the past four years I have created my signature Surf Spa Food based around the local produce, lifestyle and environment.

In this part of the world there is a temperate climate and not the extreme polarity of my hometown Melbourne's weather. Devising a menu for health retreat that was very low sugar, no dairy and focuses on creating optimal vitality for our guests came naturally in my stride once I got the hang of what replaces what such as coconut oil can replace butter in many cases.

To my delight, raw desserts often mimic their conventional counterparts with an impressive masquerade, especially when it comes to Tiramisu that has a deceptively similar texture yet slightly lighter, nuttier taste to the 'real thing'. Ultimately it's all about taste and texture when it comes to imitation.

This living 'cheesecake' is a full-flavoured little number with a creamy nut base and a deliciously tart, yet sweet raspberry finish. The hint of rosewater takes it from grassroots to restaurant sooner than you can shout 'Mullumbimby'!

Individual Raw-spberry Rose Cakes

RECIPES AND REMEDIES FROM AUSTRALIA'S LEADING SPA CHEF

Individual Raw-spberry Rose Cakes

This recipe looks tricky but I promise you it's not, so be patient as it's truly worth it.

For the base
1 cup activated almonds
1 cup pitted Medjool dates
Pinch good salt
1 tablespoon coconut oil, melted for oiling muffin tray

For the filling
3 cups cashews, soaked for 4 hours, drained
2 teaspoons organic vanilla extract
3 lemons, juice only
2/3 cup raw coconut oil, melted
2/3 cup raw light agave nectar
1 teaspoon organic apple cider vinegar
1 cup frozen raspberries
2 teaspoon rosewater
*available at Middle Eastern stores

Garnish
24 raspberries

To make the base
- Combine the first three ingredients in a food processor and blend well until the mixture resembles breadcrumbs
- Oil a 24 hole mini muffin pan – you'll need to use the silicone one so you can pop the cakes out with your hands press about 1 teaspoon of base mix into each muffin hole. Press firmly to ensure a tight base

To make the filling
- In a food processor, combine cashews, vanilla, coconut oil, agave and apple cider vinegar and blend until smooth
- Spoon about 1 teaspoon onto of the pressed made mix in each muffin hole. Smooth over. With the reaming mixture, add the raspberries and rosewater and puree until smooth
- Spoon the berry rose mix on top of each cake to make the third and final layer
- Press a frozen raspberry into the centre of each cake and freeze for at least six hours before serving

To serve
- Gently press the base of each muffin hole to help push the cakes out
- Either place on another tray and continue to freeze or serve immediately
- Garnish with more raspberries if desired

Raw Tiramisu

Nothing beats the hedonic experience of cream fats and refined sugars in non-raw desserts. Although I'd be eating towards ecstasy with regular desserts, I'd also find myself struggling in finding the control switch to stop. The experience usually ends with regret and self-blame for weakness. For some reason I can't quite explain, raw fats and sugars differ in giving their sense of satiation or fullness.

TIP: If you cannot source certain raw ingredients such as honey and cacao, don't let that hold you back. Use regular honey and roasted cacao powder (cocoa).

Cashew Milk
1 cup cashews, soaked 1-2 hours
3 cups water
2 tablespoons raw honey
1 teaspoon vanilla essence
    pinch sea salt

- Blend all ingredients in a blender on high until you reach smooth milky mixture
- Use the remaining of this milk as your raw milk substitute. Drink on its own, use with cereals, or blend into fruit shakes

Date and coconut layer
½ cup dates, pitted and soaked in ½ cup water until soft
1 cup cashews, soaked 1-2 hours
2 ½ tablespoons virgin coconut oil
1 tablespoon raw cacao powder
½ tablespoon raw honey
1 ½ teaspoons coffee extract
1 teaspoon vanilla essence
    pinch sea salt

- In a food processor, mix all ingredients until well incorporated and smooth

Cashew and coconut cream layer
1 cup cashew milk
½ young coconut, fresh meat only
1 tablespoon virgin coconut oil
1 teaspoon raw honey
½ teaspoon organic vanilla essence

- In a food processor, mix all ingredients until well incorporated and smooth

Topping
½ tablespoon raw cacao powder

RECIPES AND REMEDIES FROM AUSTRALIA'S LEADING SPA CHEF

Assembly
- In a small casserole dish or pie pan, form a cake layer (about 1cm in thickness) into the bottom of pan; then pour a layer of cream (about 0.5cm in thickness) over cake and chill in freezer until firm
- Repeat layering and refrigerate until firm
- Sift raw cacao powder to dust over top layer of cream
- Refrigerate for a few hours before serving

THE HEALING FEELING

Mastering the Art of Spa Cuisine

"The first rule of health is do not murder the food. Too high a temperature

will kill it; too low, you boil out the nutrients. You want to cook high and fast

or long and slow. The smaller you chop a vegetable,

the faster you can cook it the less it loses nutrients."

Raymond Blanc

So inspired by this newfound love of surfing I decided that it should become the backbone of my business. In 2010 I launched Surf Spa Food – a signature for my cuisine that encapsulates my food as medicine teachings and is the essence of which I will share with you in this book.

I have always been inspired by Chef Raymond Blanc whose Spa Cuisine has been celebrated for decades and helped to shape Nouvelle Cuisine and the rise of Californian cuisine. However I found interpretations of this cuisine to be overly petite, pale and unsubstantial for my audience hence Surf Spa Food was born.

My food is a long way from the *Puberty Blues* images of surfy chicks and their crotch-squeezing boyfriends who demanded "Get me a Chiko Roll".

Rice Paper Rolls with Prawns and Omelette — Makes eight

These fresh rolls are rapidly becoming more popular and are available in most Vietnamese restaurants. They are easy to prepare and can hold many different fillings. Take care when handling the delicate rice paper.

2 egg yolks, beaten

8 sheets large rice paper

1 cup cooked vermicelli noodles

12 cooked peeled and chopped prawns

1 tablespoon Vietnamese mint, chopped

½ cup shredded lettuce

1 carrot, grated

- In a non-stick omelette or crepe pan, add beaten egg yolks and heat until well cooked. Allow to cool then shred with a knife
- Dip each rice paper into some warm water so it becomes soft. Set each paper out on a clean workspace
- Distribute the noodles, omelette, prawns, mint, carrot and lettuce between the soft rice papers
- Roll the base firmly over to encase the mixture, then continue to fold over the sides and gently roll up completely
- Repeat this process with the remaining rice papers.
- Serve alone or with sweet chilli sauce

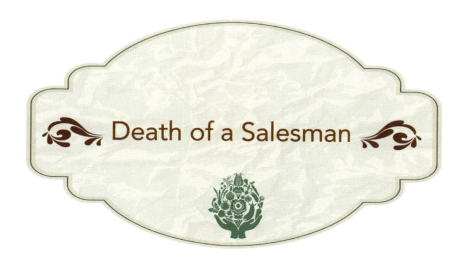

Death of a Salesman

"Being deeply loved by someone gives you strength,
while loving someone deeply gives you courage."

Lao Tzu

My dad taught me to cook, as did my maternal grandmother Evie. I grew up at the restaurant table at Jacksons, my father's first restaurant in the Melbourne suburb of Toorak. Dad thoroughly enjoyed his life ... until he realized that it was causing his death. At the peak of his smoking career - a frequent flyer who carried cartons of Peter Stuyvesant's "passport to international smoking pleasure" - he would chain smoke over a hundred cigarettes a day, lighting one after the other as he extinguished the previous one in a mammoth marble ashtray. Usually given to him as gifts during the 1970s, these ashtrays themselves could have been used as doorstops - or weapons for adulterating husbands - as they were so heavy.

Smoking was part of his persona, yet he would never light up until after his exercise regime and breakfast displaying his extraordinary discipline to his own detriment. Cigarettes with Dunhill and Cartier lighters adorned his den and dashboards. As kids we grew up engulfed in this Stuyvesant slipstream, long before medical authorities warned us and it was still acceptable to ferry children around in smoke filled cars. Back in those days real leather upholstery was used in the cars he drove which only exacerbated the stench. It's no wonder that two out of three kids took up this horrible habit. My relationship with cigarettes began in the plantation of boarding school and lasted about six years on a regular basis, then randomly for a bit longer until an extraordinary hypnotherapist guided me out of the haze.

THE HEALING FEELING

After my dad was diagnosed with cancer the first time he had pretty much given up cigarettes, fine food, wine, women, fast cars, bars ... and cigars. Two bouts of remissions couldn't tame the insidious disease despite being a tenacious ol' bugger, he hung on and fought his cancer – until his last breath one December day in 1991 at the age of 62 with nearly every cell in his body consumed by cancer.

I was devastated. Nevertheless his premature death ignited my own deep interest in healthy living, healthy food and a concern about not only my own lifestyle. So I have spent the last fifteen years studying, qualifying, researching, recipe testing and talking about wellness.

Dennis Gowing winning the Melbourne Cup on his birthday 3/11/85.
Photo courtesy of the Rennie Ellis Collection at the State Library of Victoria.

Holy Tao!

"Health is the greatest possession.

Contentment is the greatest treasure.

Confidence is the greatest friend.

Non-being is the greatest joy."

Lao Tzu

I'm a product of the seventies, born in the sixties with an avant-garde mother who also died of cigarette induced cancer in 2007. We loved Chinese food as kids – still do – and frequented The Mandarin our local restaurant every week. Somewhere between the Lazy Susan table top turner and learning Japanese language since primary school, I developed a love and respect for all things Oriental. In the Inidan summers of the 70's we would burn joss sticks and play the I Ching, the Chinese Book of Changes at my mother's house. Chinese philosophy was instilled in me from an early age and for my HSC ceramics folio I chose the ideology of the Yin and Yang. It was a pretty clumsy offering but later I went on to practice Japanese wheel thrown pottery in Fitzroy for many years with a much greater sense of style.

The principles of Chinese cosmology are known as Yin and Yang and are considered to be the most ancient Chinese idea on record. The Chinese ideogram represents balance and harmony, which dates back to the Taoist period of the sixth century. Taoism is underpinned by the Yin Yang, which gives rise to the Five Element theory that represents all of the elements in nature. According to the Tao, in everything there must be a balance of the Yin and Yang - where some of the elements that Yin represents are moon, night, cold, dark, feminine, and earth; the yang reflects their polarity - sun, day, heat, light, masculine, and heaven. Essentially, harmony of the elements is most desirable; yet achieving this balance can be rather elusive. By understanding the basic principles of Yin and Yang, it is then possible to counteract excessive or deficient patterns within the body.

The Eastern philosophy of food is that it possesses certain energies and flavours that affect our body in different ways. For example, meat, alcohol, drugs, and sugar are considered very Yang and may have an expansive or 'out there' effect on our mind and body. Consider the effects of excessive consumption of any of these and one begins to gain some understanding of the concept.

Treating a hangover with the opposing energy, that is, by consuming something contractive such as salty foods like miso soup and tamari or legumes with grains, balance will be achieved more rapidly than if one was to continue to feed the hangover with more sugar and fat, which will only create more expansive behaviour.

Chinese medicine is based on the idea that illness results from imbalances in Yin and Yang, and disruptions of the flow of vital energy, or Qi (pronounced chi). A wide variety of symptoms can occur when there is a depletion, congestion or interrupted flow. Chinese medicine employs a variety of techniques including acupuncture, herbal remedies, diet modification, moxibustion, exercise, and massage to restore the body's balance and stimulate the proper flow of Qi.

The Power of Food

"The Wise are guided by their belly rather than their eyes."

Lao Tzu

A vital formula for dealing with ill health and maintaining wellness is eating an abundance of fresh, organic, whole foods. The fewer preserved, processed and fragmented foods consumed, the more the body will thrive on the natural nutrient content in whole foods.

Processing and preserving may lengthen the shelf life and enhance the appearance of food, but certainly not for the consumer; more likely it's a short time on the shelf and a long time digesting within.

In the Western world, we have become so accustomed to consuming preservative-rich produce that we have forgotten the taste of real food. The good news is that those sweet, full-flavoured, summer berries do have a distinctive taste and smell, but only when they are chemical-free and in season.

By producing crops at certain times of the year, when our bodies most need them, nature has intended us to eat seasonally: pumpkin and potatoes in the winter, berries and stone fruit in the summer.

Unfortunately, modern science, fuelled by economic pressure, has made fruit and vegetables available throughout the year. Imagine what detrimental cultivation techniques are in process to create trans-seasonal fruit and vegetables in their off season. Combine this with a preference for highly refined carbohydrates, battery hens and nutritionally unsustainable supermarket convenience foods and the cause of our poor state of health becomes blatantly obvious.

Just look at who belongs to that supermarket trolley bursting with plastic-packaged and cardboard-coated calories. If necessary, find a mirror! A perfect match?

There is an undoubted link between industrial processing of food and degenerative diseases. In countries where there is less industrialization and the staple diet predominantly consists of mainly whole foods: nuts, seeds, legumes, fresh fruit and vegetables, research indicates that there is a lower risk of refined diet-related illnesses, which include Diabetes Type 2, Metabolic Syndrome and cancer. The cancer preventative and ameliorating role of vegetables has proven consistent, especially one rich in dark green leafy and cruciferous vegetables.

Raw Brussels Sprouts Slaw

I loved the idea of shaved Brussels sprouts so much and this my version of my mate Andy McConnell's recipe which comes with corned duck at his new restaurant called Moon Under Water in the Builders Arms Hotel, right around the corner from my old pub the Grace Darling Hotel in Collingwood.

10 baby organic Brussels sprouts
2 small Lebanese cucumbers
3 shallots, 1/2 cup peas
4 tablespoons chopped parsley
½ cup assorted sprouts
1 tablespoon activated pepitas, dried apple
Prune dressing
200g pitted prunes
3 tablespoons Dijon mustard
2 tablespoons apple cider vinegar
1 lime, zest and juice
200ml Brookfarm lemon myrtle macadamia oil
Black pepper

- Finely shave the Brussels sprouts on a mandolin or as fine as possible using a knife. Slice cucumbers into very thin discs. Peel and finely slice shallots. Add the cucumber, shallots and parsley, sprouts, dried apple. cooked peas and pepitas to Brussels sprouts and toss well – set aside
- Place prunes in a pot of water and simmer for 10–15 minutes or until completely soft. Once soft, strain the prunes and then puree prunes in a blender with remaining dressing ingredients. Spoon alongside slaw or toss through

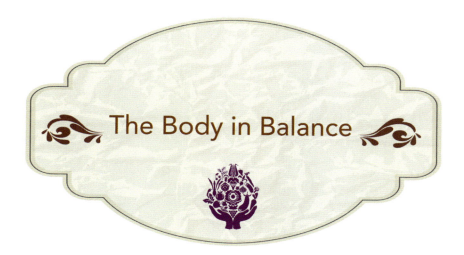

The Body in Balance

All structures of the body - organs, glands, bones, circulatory system etc, although specialised in function, are designed to work in concert. When one begins to deteriorate a note of disharmony is sounded, not only to the brain, but also to all other parts of the body via changes in the blood, alterations in glandular secretions and nerve conduction. As the metabolism shifts in response to an organ malfunction, every cell in the body is alerted to this.

Maintaining homeostasis, or balance, underlies the principle objectives of many ancient and traditional cultures. The foundations of the Chinese Yin–Yang Principles and the Ayurvedic practices of the Indian subcontinent, rest in the solid wisdom of the power of food as a healing, nurturing and life enhancing medicine. They believe that without this balance, the vital force Qi or prana will be blocked, thus causing imbalance within the body.

Ruski Wisdom

Prana: What the yogis call the life force of the body.

Piranha: A deadly Amazonian fish with sharp teeth that can cause havoc and probably a lot of blood.

Pronoia: The sneaking suspicion that the Universe is conspiring in your favour.

The Western world has been slow in embracing the fact that such a vital energy force does exist in the human body and in the foods it needs to live healthily. As we become more interconnected globally, the wisdom of the East may marry that of the West and that integrative medicine will be embraced and become the mainstream healing practice.

It is when this balance is disrupted that we become unwell. If the imbalance continues to deteriorate, cell division and tissue damage will occur causing degenerative diseases such as cancer, diabetes, heart disease and autoimmune diseases. These can only develop in unhealthy tissue in which a precancerous condition already exists. Healthy cells are aerobic, that is, they thrive on oxygen. They are also toxin free. Anaerobic cells lack oxygen and consequently have the potential to fester within a toxic environment, to differentiate, divide, deform and multiply into a cancerous growth.

When the minerals and vitamins have been extracted during the refining process such as the alevrone or outer layer of grains containing polyphenols called lignans, are removed the full nutritional component of the food is no longer valid and much cancer has been linked to an excessive intake of refined foods.

Candida Albicans was once a popular diagnosis of the late nineties, (*see chapter The Yeast Beast*). It is thought to be the result of excessive consumption and/or prolonged use of antibiotics that destroy the healthy intestinal flora. Therefore allowing the yeast to grow unimpeded in the colon and throughout the body, in severe cases.

According to Chinese medicine, a deficient state may be associated with someone who is frail and weak, or one who may have been 'burning the candle at both ends'. This state can be the result of under nourishment and may be accompanied with overall low energy and spirit. Symptoms may be pale skin; fatigue and the tongue maybe clear with a light coating.

Grill Seekers

*"Diet as a cure is now common and in many cases does
a great deal more than medicine affecting the desired result."*

Mrs. Isabella Beeton - Everyday Cookery 1861

In 1990 I became the licensee of the historic Grace Darling Hotel, on Smith Street in Collingwood. I was the Publican for eight years with my brother Chris joining me as co-manager not long after my father died. We proudly created Gowings Grace Darling Hotel – an innovative and multi-award winning dining and entertainment emporium in the inner city of Melbourne. We helped to launch the careers of bands like The Waifs and Leonardo's Bride. We offered our exclusive Sophy Blake hand-painted acoustic stage to our great friends including Vika and Linda, Nick Barker, Kerri Simpson, Dan Warner, Tracy Kingman, John McAll, Baby Lemonade and supported well-established acts including Relax with Max, Stephen Cummings and Colin Hay.

Since those days - when I was the nicest publican in town and we dished up more fish and chips than Brighton Pier - I have been studying, researching and developing healthier and more holistic alternatives to the Standard Australian Diet (no wonder it's called SAD) and styling it into my own signature Surf Spa Food brand.

So, with all the evidence based proof that trans fats are deadly, it is my heartfelt conviction that chefs, restaurateurs and hoteliers can not afford to be naive about the dangers of heating cooking oils beyond their unique flashpoints and subsequently exposing their patrons to the well-documented detrimental effects of unhealthy cooking techniques. Then offering a menu full off of highly processed, preserved foodstuffs combined with unhealthy cooking techniques. Just saying.

This may not be music to the individual's palate or a restaurateur's purse but my observations of the cancer process - and other degenerative diseases - have taught me so much about health and healing.

Especially that once you realise that feeling healthy is a different and a far superior feeling to what you experienced prior to the transition, there is certainly no going back!

My beloved brother Chris Gowing and I.

Beyond the Ladies Lounge
Australia's Female Publicans
Dr. Clare Wright

'Beyond the Ladies Lounge' challenges the myth of the Australian pub as a male domain by documenting the central role that women have historically played in hotelkeeping from colonial times to the present.

"Samantha was twenty-four years old when she took over her father's mantle as a prominent Melbourne hotelier. As an attractive, energetic, educated young woman seeking an income and an outlet for her talents at the end of the twentieth century, she could have chosen any number of professions.

She selected hotelkeeping not only because of her family connections, but also because it gave her the opportunity to have a 'public persona', 'gain notoriety', use her 'natural born' womanly inclination to be a 'provider' while at the same time 'be in the thick of things. 'As a social person', Samantha found that the job suited her inherent abilities while giving her the chance to make a difference.

But for Samantha, one of her greatest challenges was reconciling her role as an agent for change among a new generation of hotel patrons with the legacy of the 'old-style' female publican, complete with her demure attire, stately comportment and professional air of authority and reserve."

Extract from Beyond the Ladies Lounge   Melbourne University Press 2003

That Ol' Gut Feeling

Ever thought twice about crossing the street or trusting a new neighbour or colleague? Maybe you had the sense that something unusual was about to happen. Perhaps, you have read of people who chose not to get on a plane that eventually crashed, because they had a 'bad feeling'. Or, have you uttered the words, "I've had a gut full!" Well, chances are your belly was trying to tell you something that your brain upstairs could not put into words.

Our digestive system is an intricate cellular matrix of delicately integrated components, and is well documented as being the 'second brain'. It is home to over one hundred million neurons, many more than our spiny backbones. It can provide practitioners with an enormous amount of information regarding a person's overall health, energy and their emotional responses.

In Qi Gong, the gut is known as the abdominal brain. Naturopathically, we first learn how to 'fix the gut'. Nutritionally, we know that excess junk food makes us feel lousy and that comfort food cheers us up. But with the right approach, healthy food can actually provide us with an abundance of vitality and energy.

Butterflies, nerves and nausea, even a woman's intuition, may be a subliminal function of the Enteric Nervous System (ENS). However, the clinical diagnosis of Irritable Bowel Syndrome has recently served as a banner band-aid for a belly full of discomforting symptoms, stress-related illnesses and worse, disease. The role of the ENS is to regulate the normal digestive activity of the digestive system and prepare it for whatever its future may hold.

Like its spiny cousin the Central Nervous System, your ENS is a thriving population of healthy Intestinal Flower Power that loves to transmit and process messages from those diverse and unique bubbling hotspots: cells and circuits, neurons and neurotransmitters.

The stress phenomenon is not specific; it is an all-encompassing umbrella complex that reaches out to every demographic on the planet and may be triggered by an emotional, environmental or physical response to a wide variety of stimuli. However, stress is also an energetic force that can be turned into a positive, powerful motivational tool when channelled appropriately. It is imperative to remember that stress is predominantly our emotional reaction to a difficult situation that may then manifest in the physical body as a sign or symptom of poor health.

Had a Gut Full?

How stress depletes the body of its vital resources is a complex and intricate mechanism. Typically, the neural-transit and hormonal highways are tested to their limits, as they react with their 'fight or flight' responses. The bulk of the energy comes from the adrenal glands, which nestle snugly upon each kidney and produce the adrenaline hormone. A constant stress reaction will ultimately see a decline in the amount of readily available adrenaline, thus resulting in energy burn out.

Ever woken up and felt like you could still sleep for a week? Find yourself reaching for a power drink or a chocolate bar at 3pm? Just feel like you don't have as much energy as you should? Chances are you're experiencing energy burn out.

In Chinese medicine, this may be diagnosed as 'Deficient Kidney Yang'. In the West, it earns the unfair nickname of 'yuppie flu', or Chronic Fatigue Syndrome, but it is anything but a seasonal virus. Unlike flu symptoms that go away in a few days or weeks, CFS symptoms can hang on, or come and go frequently for months, if not years. You might bear this in mind the next time you reach for your next cup of coffee and accompanying cigarette to manage that deadline ... the worst-case scenario may result in you being the dead line!

It's not just the black stuff, those pesky power drinks – c'mon, you know the ones – are more potent that any heart starter I know and do the most dreadful things to the kidney energy, not to mention the abrasive and acidic effect they have on the intestinal walls.

Beating those Underbelly Blues

For many years I taught yoga asana and clinical Pilates, retiring when I broke my right knee in 2010. I took it as a sign to focus on my culinary path. I still practice both regularly for postural realignment and stress release. Awareness practice such as these and also Qi Gong stabilize the response of the nervous system to stress, removing the constant muscular tension produced by the repeated alerts from the central nervous system and calming the involuntary symptoms of threat: the racing heart, sweating, anxiety - all roused by the Sympathetic Nervous System.

A healthy nervous system enables muscles, organs and tissues of the body to work at full efficiency and gives sharper sensory perception. It also creates a sense of vitality and energy.

Bundles of fibres form the larger nerves of the body benefit stretching and cleansing with each pose. By clearing toxins from these tissues, the poses benefit neurotransmissions at the fine nerve endings and at the synapses between the nerves. One of the monoamine neurotransmitters called dopamine (DA) is responsible for reward-driven learning and is kinda like the smiley face of the brain world in that it makes you feel good. Like serotonin, the better known neurotransmitter, dopamine depletion can be the result of drug use – particularly cocaine and amphetamines – and is also linked to the nervous system condition Parkinson's disease which is due to the loss of dopamine secreting neurons and causes impaired movement and tremors.

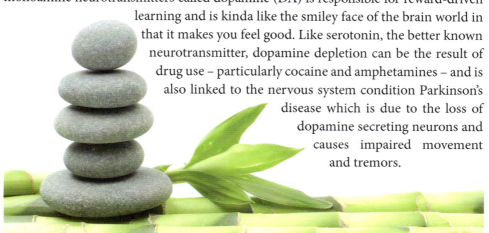

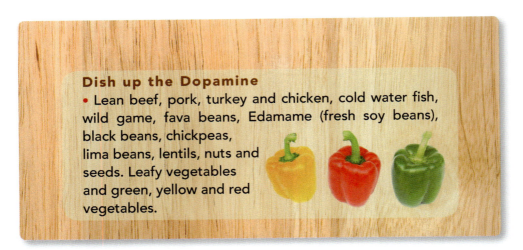

Dish up the Dopamine
• Lean beef, pork, turkey and chicken, cold water fish, wild game, fava beans, Edamame (fresh soy beans), black beans, chickpeas, lima beans, lentils, nuts and seeds. Leafy vegetables and green, yellow and red vegetables.

Postures to calm the mind

- Inverted postures such as shoulder stands have a cooling effect on the body. They also stimulate the Parasympathetic Nervous System, which helps to calm, relax and soothe the mind and body. Here, the spinal nerves leave the cord in pairs from either side of each segment and branch finely to form the parasympathetic nervous, or the peripheral system. Relax!

- Forwards bends are known for their calming effects on the mind and the nervous system. They encourage relaxation and help to decrease mood swings and irritability. Not to be done while driving

- Spinal twists and backbends stimulate the kidneys and adrenals and provide alternate sources of estrogen in the body which is useful if you are a woman, but as any bloke would know, too much estrogen in a girl can make her go a little koo koo! This is why I am so wary of estrogenic foods like unfermented soy – especially soymilk

- Pelvic floor exercises tone and increase circulation to the entire pelvic floor. They can also trigger the contraction of the transverse abdominus muscle, the deep underbelly corset that is the foundation of core stability and lower back strengthening.
Basically, if you're a girl, the tighter your inner bits are, the better the orgasm. Orgasms give oxygen to the brain and the body loves oxygen, especially in the war against cancer. So find yaself a hottie and get breathing heavy!

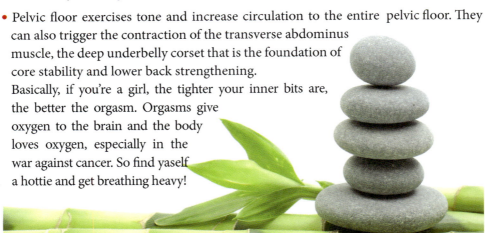

Important Foods To Calm A Nervous System

Oats are prized for their high levels of magnesium, the anti-stress mineral and their slow releasing, carbohydrate qualities that provide the body with energy throughout the day.

Carrot, beetroot and cucumber juice is a highly alkalising blend that enhances nervous function, while also supporting the kidneys by clearing excess acidity that is typically associated with increased stress levels.

Mung Beans, according to Chinese medicine, have healing properties that are highly detoxifying and cleansing. The Chinese revere them even more for their medicinal prowess than their culinary capacity, especially in decreasing the levels of triglycerides from the blood. Mung beans provide support for the body's cardiovascular system and reduce overall toxicity.

Turkey contains tryptophan, which is an essential amino acid that helps the body produce the B vitamin niacin, which in turn helps the body produces the neurotransmitter serotonin, a calming agent in the brain.

EFA's Essential Fatty Acids, most importantly, Omega 3, are found in oily fish such as: tuna, salmon, sardines and flax seeds. Macadamia oil is good too and rich in omega 7.

Pecan Nuts provide an abundance of organic pyridoxine (vitamin B6), essential for the pathways to serotonin release and nervous system health.
Eat 10-15 Pecan nuts each day.

Lecithin is a fundamental building block of brain and nerve tissue.

Wheatgrass possesses highly concentrated enzymes such as super oxide dismutase (SOD), a powerful anti-aging antioxidant that can slow down the effects of potentially carcinogenic molecules and help to neutralise free radical exposure on the cells.

Seasonal Recipes for a Nervous System

"Winter wheat, the grain is groaning on the stem."

Michelle Shocked

Traditional Chinese Medicine suggests that to keep the winter chill out we should enjoy an abundance of 'warming' food. These ingredients have a healing effect on our bodies by heating our internals and keeping the cold at bay. Chestnuts, aduki beans, quinoa, pumpkin, lima beans, ginger and shiitake mushrooms have warming properties and may also help to dry our systems of unwelcome cold symptoms so prevalent during winter.

Wontons of Roasted Chestnut, Ginger and Aduki Beans

Makes 24 wontons

100 grams fresh chestnuts
30 grams fresh ginger root, minced
50 grams aduki beans, soaked overnight
3 tablespoons tamari
2 teaspoons sesame seeds
6 spring onions, finely chopped
24 wonton wrappers

- Preheat oven to 220 C. Place chestnuts on baking tray and bake for about 30 minutes. Allow to cool then peel and discard skins. Cook aduki beans in plenty of boiling water for 30 minutes or until soft. Allow to cool. Process chestnut flesh with aduki beans, ginger, tamari, spring onion and sesame seeds. Combine well

- Separate wonton wrappers and place a teaspoon of the filling in the middle of each wrapper. Gather the corners together and carefully press together to seal. Place wontons in a bamboo steamer over boiling water. Cover with bamboo lid and steam for about 5 minutes. Serve with coriander dipping sauce

Coriander dipping sauce
½ bunch coriander
½ cup tamari
¼ lemon juice
1 teaspoon grain mustard

- Combine all ingredients together in a blender

Aduki, Pumpkin & Coconut Curry

Serves 4

- 225 gm aduki beans, soaked eight hours, rinsed and drained
- Pinch of seaweed – arame, wakame, hijiki
- 2 tablespoons of coconut oil
- 1 x Spanish onion, diced finely
- 1 teaspoon mustard seeds
- ½ teaspoon cumin seeds
- 1 x tin 400ml coconut cream
- 1 teaspoon tomato paste
- 2 x green chillies, seed removed, chopped finely
- 200gm pumpkin, skin & seed removed, cut into 2cm dice
- ¼ teaspoon ground coriander
- ¼ teaspoon ground cumin
- 2 x cup water or vegetable stock
- 2-4 x handfuls spinach leaves, washed & dried

- Cook aduki beans in plenty of water with a pinch of seaweed to detoxify the beans. Cook until tender, about 30-40 minutes. Ensure the pot does not dry out
- Heat the oil and sauté the onion, mustard seeds & cumin seeds until they pop
- Transfer cooked onions, cumin and mustard seeds into a thick-based large casserole pot
- Add aduki, tomato paste, coconut cream, ground spices, chillies, diced pumpkin
- Add water and bring to the boil then simmer 20-25 minutes until the pumpkin is cooked through
- Add spinach and gently wilt taking care while mixing not to break up the pumpkin

RECIPES AND REMEDIES FROM AUSTRALIA'S LEADING SPA CHEF

Spring

Spring heralds renewal and cleansing. In Chinese medicine it represents liver energy and the primary function of the liver is detoxification. Your liver's job is to cleanse and filter the blood and promote the elimination of toxins, hormones and to facilitate digestion. The liver governs fat metabolism by releasing lipids and associated toxins into the blood for elimination. Circles under the eyes, headaches, weight gain, nausea, mood swings and bad breath are all signs of an overloaded liver.

Did you know that if you love your liver a little bit more you'd have greater success losing weight?

Lymphatic Tisane

A tisane is a herbal infusion of leaves and flowers, steeped for a few minutes so as to release the essential oils. I have created this fragrant, subtle blend of leaves and flowers, collectively known as lymphagogues, to help clear my lymphatic system after a gentle spring liquid cleanse of juices, smoothies and vegetable broth cooked at a very low temperature. I have noticed during my cleanse that the lymph nodes around the hairline at the back of my neck and under my ears were inflamed, so each ingredient has been carefully selected for its immune boosting or lymph clearing properties to alleviate my symptoms.

Lymphatic Tisane

¼ cup cleavers

¼ cup calendula flowers

¼ cup echinacea

- Combine herbs and leaves in a mixing bowl then transfer to an airtight container
- In a large teapot, place 2 teaspoon of the tisane blend and cover with hot water. Allow to steep for five minutes before drinking

Disclaimer: I am not a herbalist, just a clinical nutritionist so be sure to get a professional opinion before embarking on any healing journey. Therefore take this tea in moderation and observe your reactions carefully

The Beauty of the Beets

Beets have strong detoxifying properties and they are high in chlorine, which assists in the cleansing of the liver, kidneys and bloodstream. They are also rich in potassium, which balances the metabolism and in vitamin C, vital for efficient alcohol breakdown in the body. Beets contain betaine, which promotes the regeneration of liver cells and the flow of bile and promotes beneficial effect on fat metabolism. Lemon juice promotes liver function by creating an alkalising effect of the system once digested and alfalfa sprouts help to breakdown toxicity in the liver by alkalising the blood. A pinch of fresh chilli will activate peripheral circulation to get things moving again. The honey neutralises alcohol and sweetens the mix.

Beetroot, Pomegranate & Rosewater Salad

Serves 8 as a side
This recipe works best with a Thermomix

3 large beetroot
35 grams olive oil
10 grams rosewater
Juice of 1 lemon
Cracked pepper, to taste
10 grams chives
10 grams mint leaves
10 grams parsley leaves
10 grams lime leaves, shredded
80 grams activated pepitas
1 small pomegranate, seeds removed

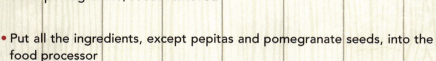

- Put all the ingredients, except pepitas and pomegranate seeds, into the food processor

- Chop at 5 in the TM or about 20 in your food processor. Then scrape down. Chop for another 20 seconds being careful not to over-process the mix

- Spoon onto a serving platter and scatter over the pepitas and pomegranate seeds

Thanks to Dani Valent for the inspiration for this recipe

Zenergising Beet Top Tea

If your liver's a-quiver, this tonic will deliver!

2 beetroots, washed and cut up
1 lemon, washed with the rind only removed (keep the pith)
1 cup of alfalfa sprouts, rinsed and dried
1 inch piece of ginger, peeled
¼ chilli
1-2 teaspoons of honey

- Place beetroot, lemon, alfalfa, chilli and ginger in a vegetable juicer and process. Stir in honey and enjoy.

Other foods to enjoy for a lovelier liver

Lemon Juice: In water, lemon juice has a slightly laxative effect and stimulates the digestive juices. Squeeze half a lemon into warm water and drink immediately after rising in the morning is the foundation drink for a long and healthy life.

Artichokes: Contain plant compounds known as caffeoylquinic acids, which increase the flow of bile and help to digest fats.

Onions and Garlic: Both are rich in sulphur – containing compounds, which help to eliminate harmful heavy metals from the body.

Protein: This is required by the liver for the detoxification process.

RECIPES AND REMEDIES FROM AUSTRALIA'S LEADING SPA CHEF

Shoots and seeds are the epitome of a new life, unadulterated, innocent and unblemished. When they sprout, they are living organisms, so by ingesting such vital or living energy we are consuming a whole food that has not been through the trauma of process. Therefore it is still alive and contains the maximum potential for nutrient content.

Salad of Shoots, Nuts, Peas and Leaves with Red Quinoa

1 cup red quinoa, rinsed and drained
1 cup water
100 grams assorted sprouts – mung, snowpea, mustard cress
50 grams green peas, cooked
1 tablespoon mint, finely shredded
50 grams raw almonds, roughly chopped
1 teaspoon linseeds, lightly crushed

Dressing
4 tablespoons cup extra virgin olive oil
1 tablespoon apple cider vinegar
1 lime, zest and juice
Cracked black pepper

- Place quinoa in a saucepan and cover with 1 cup of water. Bring to the boil, reduce heat and simmer gently without the lid until nearly all of the liquid has been absorbed

- Cover pot with a folded tea towel and then place lid so as to absorb remaining liquid and the quinoa has started to split from the husk and become slightly translucent. Fluff it with a fork

- Combine sprouts, peas and mint leaves, almonds and linseeds with cooked quinoa

- Whisk dressing ingredients together well and gently toss through the salad

THE HEALING FEELING

For rice and quinoa

I discovered the tea towel method when I was working at Minami Japanese restaurant as they would complete absorption method rice this way. Cover pot with a folded tea towel and then place lid so as to absorb remaining liquid until all of the water has been absorbed. This will create a steam effect and also keep your rice or quinoa warm until serving. Once complete, fluff it with a fork.

Why I activate nuts and seeds

I activate our nuts and seeds in a special oven called a dehydrator, which slowly dries out ingredients so as to inhibit the growth of microorganisms and prevents the decay of the valuable nutrients. Usually the nuts and seeds have been soaked for up to 24 hours before so as to reignite the powerful enzymes they possess which can die off once they have been shelled. Dehydration takes 24-48 hours depending on the ingredient and temperature, which can be as low as 40 C.

Therapeutic Notes

Black sesame seeds are one of the highest sources of calcium and are considered a good tonic in Chinese medicine as they are lubricating to the intestines and major organs. The paler seeds have a general tonifying effect on the body overall and are especially helpful in treating dry coughs and asthma. In general, they can have a calming effect.

Did you know that they are a remedy for greying hair?

RECIPES AND REMEDIES FROM AUSTRALIA'S LEADING SPA CHEF

Gomasio

Gomasio is the principal table condiment in the Macrobiotic way of natural foods diet. Use it in lieu of salt to season your food at table, giving hearty delicious taste. Gomasio also functions as a medicine in itself. Due to its powerful ant-acid biochemical effect it strengthens digestion and improves energy immediately.

¼ cup raw, unhulled sesame seeds – black or white
1 teaspoon organic salt
¼ cup dulse flakes

- Place seeds in a clean, dry, frying pan and toast on low heat, stirring often until they start to pop

- In a mortar and pestle or coffee grinder, combine salt, seeds and dulse

Sunny Sunflower Whip

1 cup of sunflower seeds
½ cup of lemon juice
2 garlic cloves
½ cup of tahini
1-2 tablespoons of tamari
1 teaspoon of cumin seeds
Pinch of cayenne

- Put all ingredients through a food processor and mix to a paste

Autumn

Figs

Figs are one of the sexiest fruits on the planet. These plump, soft, sweet, luscious beauties come from one variety of the Fichus tree, which probably originated in Asia Minor. It is one of the oldest, edible plants. Serve figs with sliced melon or pears and prosciutto as an appetizer.

Useless Fact

My friend Ruski who helped to edit this book reckons he had a fig tree in his house and so did the two corporate BMW-driving dog-owning lesbians next door. Their figs always tasted better than his. Go figure!

Figs are a natural laxative and their tiny seeds assist the colon in processing toxic waste. Rhubarb is considered a bitter 'fire' food, which tends to dry the system, balance excess dampness and promote elimination.

Autumn Rolls of Fig and Rhubarb with Rhubarb Puree

Serves 4

12 medium ripe figs, quartered
100ml pear juice concentrate
1 ½ cups of water
Zest of 1 lemon
1 bunch of fresh rhubarb
1 packet rice paper rounds, small
1 tablespoon coconut oil, melted for brushing the rolls pre baking
Extra figs for garnish, if desired

- Preheat oven to 200 C
  Combine pear juice concentrate, zest and water and bring to the boil. Reduce heat, add figs and poach for about 10 minutes
- Remove figs from syrup with slotted spoon. Continue to reduce syrup for 30 minutes on low heat to about 2/3 cup until it coats the back of a spoon
- Wash rhubarb stalks and discard poisonous leaves. Slice rhubarb into 3-cm. pieces and add to reserved fig syrup. Place lid on saucepan and simmer over moderate heat for 5 minutes until tender
- Add 1 cup of rhubarb to the fig mixture to bind. Blend remaining rhubarb puree with a little reduced syrup and process until smooth enough to pour
- Place a dessertspoon of fruit in the centre of a rice paper roll wrapper and roll up diagonally, tucking in the sides as you go. Seal with a little coconut oil and brush some over each roll
- Bake for 10-15 minutes until golden

The Yeast Beast

Our digestive system houses recurring yeast called *Candida Albicans* which helps produce energy and facilitates digestion. It exists naturally on the skin and inside the digestive, respiratory and reproductive organs. However it can affect any organ in the body and is the most common cause of Candidiasis often from prolonged of use of broad-spectrum antibiotics, steroids, the oral contraceptive pill, excessive stress and over-consumption of sugar and dairy products. This can exacerbate the production of yeast.

> **Candida** loves sugar and all things yeasty – think fermentation of alcohol or sourdough bread - therefore it thrives in this environment and will send messages to the brain often resulting in uncontrollable sugar cravings – either simple CHO such as fruit, fruit juice, sweets and chocolate or more complex CHO cravings for the starch and yeast found in breads and pastries.

If left unchecked, the yeast overgrowth within the gut colonises and multiplies giving rise to bloating, flatulence, abdominal pain, burping, constipation, diarrhoea, malaise and fatigue. Symptoms may also include dandruff, swimmer's ear, athlete's foot, oral and vaginal thrush, fungal rashes, rectal itching, joint pain and inability to concentrate, brain fog, mood swings and depression. Sound familiar? For many years Candida was a diagnostic buzzword – a trendy name for the umbrella of symptoms that seemed to brand most females within the community. Certainly it has its fair share of authentic diagnosis, however there maybe a differential diagnosis that goes under the radar, so be sure to see your health care professional for an accurate appraisal. The traditional Candida diet is so restrictive and I know of patients who have been on it for months with no real change. Essentially give up the sugar and the grains for a bit and listen to your gut!

Pathogenesis

Mycology is the study of fungus. Candida is a dimorphic (two shaped) fungus that can spread to all parts of the body and manifest in many different ways. This fungus grows in two ways – an ellipsoid bud and in hyphal form – it can switch from being a yeast to hyphal mode where it becomes threadlike filaments called hyphae (pronounced high fee) that form the mycelium of a fungus – where the fungus interconnects to form a greenish blanket on a mouldy orange or piece of mouldy bread. Then this hyphae spreads from the tips and it's these tips that are quite penetrable and can permeate into the skin and intertwine with digestive fibres and tracts. How hideous is that?

So when the mould undergoes a pathogenical transformation into the fungal form the hyphae penetrates – or burrows - through the lining of the gut, potentially forming roots and entering the rest of the body causing extensive tissue damage throughout, also known as yeast tissue penetration.

As the yeast overgrows it creates an increase in the colonisation within the oral, vaginal and intestinal cavities. Not all thrush is Candida – it may be parasitical, viral or bacterial or a reaction to humidity, sex, exercise, tight clothing or cyclic discharge. It can also be very common for women in their third trimester of pregnancy and patients with Diabetes Mellitus II tend to suffer from bouts of oral thrush.

The Kingdom of Fungus

In his controversial book, Cancer is a Fungus (Edizoni Lampis 2007), oncologist Dr. T. Simoncini discusses the life of the fungi. "Yeast and moulds belong to a broader family of life called fungus, one of the very few "Kingdoms" of life (other Kingdoms include plants, animals and bacteria)." There are over 40,000 types of funghi including mildew, bread mould, mushrooms and toadstools and rusts. Most funghi are decomposers and feed on the remains by releasing toxins to digest.

THE HEALING FEELING

So picture this. If you have an overgrowth of Candida Albicans, possibly fuelled by stress, a course of broad spectrum antibiotics for a flu or unshakable cold, continue with our diet rich in fermented things (wine, beer, sourdough bread), sugar, add a cup or two of complex carbohydrates like rice and pasta and then let it breakdown into simple sugars for a bit.

Observe these foods as they sit in your sluggish gut, add another serving of stress and watch the yeast rise (expand) and the fungus spread, creating havoc in your body including inflammatory responses such as arthritis and adrenal fatigue, auto-immune diseases, diabetes, weight gain, bloating, flatulence. You get the picture?

Is this one of the reasons why we are tired all the time?

Yeast free foods to include

Nuts & Seeds	Fresh Vegetables	Avoid all fruit 2-4 weeks
(Unprocessed)	Asparagus	(Unprocessed)
Almonds	Beets	Apple
Brazil	Broccoli	Avocado
Cashews	Brussels Sprouts	Banana
Hazelnuts	Beans	Peach
Pecans	Carrots	Pear
Pumpkin Seeds	Cauliflower	Apricot
	Celery	Grapefruit
	Lettuce	Mango
	Onions	Nectarine
	Parsley	Orange
	Peas	Papaya
	Cabbage	Pineapple
	Tomatoes	
Oils - Cold Pressed	Summer squash	**Grains & Seeds**
Almond	Eggplant	Quinoa
Avocado	Red Potatoes	Barley
Apricot	Cucumbers	Rye
Linseed	Zucchini	Oats
Olive	Green Peppers	Rice
Sesame	Squash	Millet
Butter	Winter Squash	
Macadamia	Greens	
Meat & Eggs	Turnip	**Fresh Fish**
Organic & Biodynamic	Spinach	Preferably local,
Avoid all processed	Mustard	deep sea and line-caught
meats due to the	Kale	
nitrates and nitrites	Radishes	
	Okra	
	Parnship	

Kelp Is On Its Way

Having long being a source of great healing properties in the East since 3000 BC, contemporary cuisine has begun to embrace these mineral rich marine algae with abundance. They possess a highly concentrated source of nutrients, including high protein and iron content, with high levels of manganese, potassium, phosphorous, sodium, zinc and calcium.

Hijiki and nori seaweeds contain sizable amounts of vitamin A, B, C & D and are one of the few plant foods to produce vitamin B12, making it an excellent addition to a vegan diet.

Nori is extremely high in protein and may also be used crumbled over salads and soups, while hijiki is rich in fibre, iron and calcium and has a sweet delicate flavour.

They are considered to be contractive and have an alkalising effect on the blood and "contain mucilaginous gels which have a rejuvenating effect on the lungs and gastrointestinal tract".

Miso Miscellany

One acre of land planted in soybeans produces over 20 times more useable protein than if it were used to raise beef cattle or grow their fodder.

Facts

Miso is a thick paste made by combining soybeans and barley or wheat or rice (or a mixture of these grains) with a yeast mould (koji) that has been cultivated from a soybean, barley or rice base. The mixture is then aged from three months to three years. Consider the potential number of combinations this set of variables provides and you'll get a sense of the wide range of colours, tastes and textures available out there in miso-land. Miso is very nutritious and is a basic element of many Japanese soups, stews and braised dishes.

Aka miso – also known as sendai-miso, inaka-miso and red miso – is a rich paste made from barley with a strong, salty flavour. Hatcho miso is a very pungent, salty variation, with a thick, grainy texture and a dark, murky colour. It is made from only soybeans and is used in small amounts to add richness to soups and broths. Shinshu miso is a golden-yellow, all-purpose version of this paste. It has a mellow flavour and a rather high salt content. Miso has a sweet, creamy, nutty flavour and a cooling thermal nature.

5 things to do with miso

1. Whisk barley (mugi) miso in to steaming dashi stock. Add cooked ramen noodles and fresh shiitake mushrooms for a provincial Japanese meal

2. Blend red (aka) miso with mirin, black sesame seeds and ginger juice to dress hot pumpkin

3. Make miso topping for grilled eggplant. Gently simmer white (shiru) miso with egg yolks, sake, mirin, sugar and dashi stock until thick. Spoon over eggplant

4. Hatcho miso (organic & unpasteurised) and is an excellent medicinal, hardy, deep robust miso and can be used mixed together with water, hone and sesame oil and pour over cooked spinach

5. Combine equal amounts of brown rice (genmai) miso and sake and serve as a dipping sauce for grilled chicken or tofu skewers

1 thing not to do!

1. Never let miso boil, as it will lose aroma and flavour

Ume-sho-kuzu

Ume-sho-kuzu is one of the most widely prescribed Japanese macrobiotic home remedies. It is made from kuzu, umeboshi, a pickled sour plum and shoyu. Kuzu is the root of a Japanese plant like arrowroot, which grows wild in mountainous regions. This tonic helps to strengthen the blood, improve circulation, restore energy and promote good digestion. Great for sore throats, coughs colds and itchy holes, it also supports most Yin conditions and helps to balance yang excess such as hangovers. Organic kuzu is a high quality ingredient that is an ideal thickening agent for soups and stews, in both sweet and savoury dishes. In Japan, kuzu has long been held in high regard for its ability to help alkaline the body.

1 teaspoon kuzu starch
1 umeboshi plum or 1 teaspoon umeboshi paste
½ teaspoon freshly grated ginger
A few drops shoyu
½ lemon, juice only

- In a small bowl, place the umeboshi plum and add 4 or 5 drops of shoyu – set aside
- In a small saucepan, bring slightly less than one cup of water to the boil over medium heat. Best to use non-metallic saucepan, such as ceramic, glass or enamel-coated
- Dissolve the kuzu in a bit of cold water and pour into the hot water. Whisk gently to prevent lumps from forming
- As soon as the mixture changes colour – from chalky white to translucent – about ½ to one minute, then remove from heat
- Place the umeboshi/shoyu in a teapot together with a small amount of freshly grated ginger and a squeeze of lemon
- Pour kuzu mix over the umeboshi / shoyu, strain and drink while hot

Umeboshi

Umeboshi plums are traditional Japanese salted plums but are more closely related to the apricot. They are a popular kind of tsukemono (pickles) and are extremely sour and salty. They are part of the Zen macrobiotic diet and help to balance sugar cravings and centre the emotions.

Ume-sho-kuzu

A Japanese Fun Guy

In the New York Times' *Food Encyclopaedia*, Craig Claiborne shares the romantic notion that, "the ancients believed that mushrooms were created by thunderbolts, possibly because they flourished after rain."

French horticulturalists pioneered mushroom reproduction and today mushroom cultivation stands as a thriving industry, offering an abundance of species available in autumn and throughout the year.

The Japanese Shiitake mushrooms are the second most-consumed mushrooms in the world. They have a pungent, woody flavour with a sweet, meaty texture. In the thermal energetics of Chinese medicine, they are neutral, sweet and drying. Like adzuki beans,

shiitake have an absorbent property, which makes them suitable for drying damp conditions such as Candida. They are also helpful for decreasing cholesterol and lowering high blood pressure.

In the mid-eighties, the Japanese government approved a new product featuring Shiitake for the treatment of stomach and cervical cancers. Concentrated forms of letinan, a shiitake extract, treat cancer, AIDS, diabetes, fibrocystic breast disease and other conditions with impressive results. Nutritionally, they fight viruses, lower cholesterol and regulate blood pressure.

Funky Fungus Facts

Shiitake contain all eight of the essential amino acids and they are also rich in vitamin B12, Cobalamin, predominantly found in animal protein, an energy-boosting vitamin that is so often lacking in the vegetarian diet. They have natural antiviral and immune boosting properties and contain a sizeable amount of the protein, interferon that aids in building immunity against cancer.

Shiitake mushrooms are grown commercially by inoculating the cut logs of a particular 'sporing' oak tree. Their seasons are typically autumn and spring. Externally, fresh shiitake are dark brown with smooth, velvety caps housing a fluffy fawn to pink flesh, with a slightly spongy texture. Discard any hard stems before cooking and store them in a brown paper bag in a dark place, or keep in the drawer of the refrigerator for up to 2-3 weeks. Dried shiitake can be quite pungent, tough and overbearing and they're often sprayed with chemicals to facilitate the drying and packaging processes.

Probiotics - Acidophilus & Bifidus

Probiotics stimulate the growth of microorganisms such as the friendly bacteria that help to re-inoculate your gut micro flora. This facilitates digestion to create a healthy gastric environment. Three primary bacterial strains are key including lactobacillus acidophilus, bifidus and bulgaricus.

Lactobacillus acidophilus contains powerful antibiotic properties. Milk is inoculated with bacteria to create the process of fermentation, which in turn coagulates the milk into lactic acid to create yoghurt. Friendly bacteria such as Lactobacillus acidophilus and Bifidobacterium thrive in a high fibre environment such as your large intestine, which enhances bacterial growth.

Did you know that yoghurt is touted as an all-round health food however it can be contraindicated in those who suffer from arthritis? Also, sweetening your yoghurt with honey – a natural antibiotic – will kill off yoghurt enzymes and bacteria.

RECIPES AND REMEDIES FROM AUSTRALIA'S LEADING SPA CHEF

The Digestive Detective

The bifido bacteria is like your digestive detective, ready to combat potential pathogenic invaders from moving into your intestine, taking over and unleashing a biological bacteria warfare that can diminish your intestinal functions and create an assortment of disorders.

Yoghurt Recipe
Berry Manilow

200 g raspberries
200 g blueberries
500 ml organic yoghurt
Honey optional

- Stir through to combine and drizzle with honey
- Serve with strong voice!

Digestive enzymes play an important role in facilitating freedom from flatulence and other feisty functions. Incomplete digestion may be a contributing factor in the development of many ailments including flatulence, bloating, belching, food allergies, nausea, bad breath, bowel problems and stomach disorders.

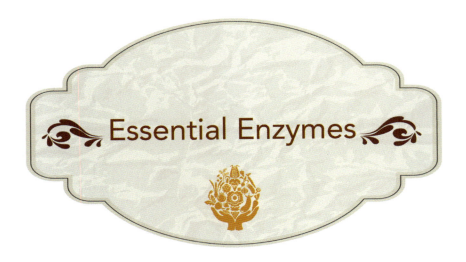

Essential Enzymes

Deficient secretion of HCL signs may include:	
Bloating	Food allergies
Belching	Chronic intestinal parasites
Flatulence	Abnormal flora
Nausea	Peeling and cracked fingernails
Indigestion	A sense of fullness immediately after meals
Constipation	Undigested food in stool
Diarrhoea	Anaemia
	* Folic acid, vitamin B12 and iron will not be absorbed if there is too little acid

The role of hydrochloric acid is to prohibit unfriendly bacteria from colonising and multiplying. HCL hydrochloric acid stimulates pancreatic secretion, activates pepsin and sterilizes the stomach from bacteria and parasites.

RECIPES AND REMEDIES FROM AUSTRALIA'S LEADING SPA CHEF

Role of selected enzymes and HCL in the body

ENZYME	ROLE
AMYLASE (pancreas)	• Breaks down carbohydrates Sucrose, Maltose • Found in saliva
PROTEASE (pancreas)	• Breaks down protein into amino acids Responsible parasite control in the small intestine - Intestinal worms - Yeast overgrowth - Bacteria
LIPASE (pancreas)	• Breaks down fats into fatty acids and glycerol
PANCREATIN (pancreas)	• Contains protease, amylase and lipase;- functions in the intestine and in the blood
BROMELAIN	• Extracted from pineapple plant, helps break down proteins
PAPAIN	• Extracted from papaya fruit • Aids in protein digestion
LACTASE	• Breaks down lactose found in milk products
PEPSIN	• Breaks down proteins • Function depends on availability of HCL
HCL	• Hydrochloric acid stimulates pancreatic secretion • Activates pepsin and sterilizes the stomach from bacteria and parasites

It is easy to love the people far away.
It is not always easy to love those close to us.
It is easier to give a cup of rice to relieve hunger
than to relieve the loneliness and pain of someone unloved in our own home.

Mother Theresa

The Controversial Grain

Wheat (Triticum aestivum)

Wheat covers more of our planet than any other crop and it has laid the foundation for much of our Western diet. Supermarket shelves are stacked with colourful bundles of sliced bread, all wrapped up like Christmas bonbon - complete with those cheap gifts - the additives, or synthetic versions of the nutrients destroyed by the processing – in particular, Thiamine B1, Riboflavin B2, Niacin B3 and fibre.

Further, down the aisles, in the pasta section, there are rows of different shaped and coloured wheat pastas. Many people are under the impression that diversity of pasta shapes and colours means diversity of nutritional values. Basically, there is no difference. They have the same inflammatory effect on the small intestine for 3.9% of the population, thanks to the gliadin content of gluten.

Wheat, barley, oats and rye all contain gluten, which is the combination of the proteins, gliadin and glutenin. While the other grains contain smaller amounts, wheat is the main source. Remember that paste we made out of flour and water as kids that we called glue? Well it has the same adhesive properties as gluten.

It is not surprising that gluten has been identified as the major contributor of Celiac disease for the 3.9% of the population mentioned above. Those with this disease are unable to absorb and digest through the jejunum of the small intestine- a sticky situation, indeed! Gliadin is also associated with allergic reactions of the skin such as dermatitis and psoriasis.

Awareness of wheat intolerance is on the rise and the market is responding with many attractive gluten-free alternatives.

For those who have no trouble digesting this prolific grain, wheat can be the source of much satisfaction. Certainly its derivatives can be extremely beneficial whether in the form of wheat germ and its oil.

Wheat germ is 3% of wheat grain – just the root and shoot (hey that sounds like something you wanna do to a cheating lover!). It is the most nutritious component, containing iron, phosphorous, sodium, chromium, potassium and magnesium, as well as vitamins B1, B6, E, K and inositol.

Wheatgrass is the pre-grain wheat shoot, which means that it contains all the nutrients required for the formation of the grain - calcium, magnesium, iron, vitamins A and C - and it is a vital source of chlorophyll.

Ideally, wheatgrass should be consumed as a juice that has been freshly extracted by pressing the live wheatgrass. The recommended dosage is 30ml per day. Dilute it with filtered water or fresh apple juice, or simply enjoy it 'straight'. It is, however, an acquired taste.

The Wealth of Wheatgrass

Jocund juice joints across the land are bountiful with spiky trays of wheatgrass, gently waving their nutritious blades. Whilst it may seem that this is a new fad, wheatgrass and its juice have been available for some time.

Juice bars have been dealing in the commodity of wheatgrass since the 1980s, injecting us with the living light of plants. Some enthusiasts have embraced this pasture with all the fervour of a Jersey cow, whilst others are less reverent - usually being put off by its pungent odour of a freshly mowed lawn. What we are discovering is what our farmyard friends have known all along - that grass is good.

The medicinal use of grasses and chlorophyll date back to the Bible and has been used widely ever since. Grass poultices are been used for their cooling properties to treat inflammation, burns, itchiness and eyestrain. Nutritionally, wheatgrass possesses high protein levels similar to most meat and also has traces of vitamin B12. Therefore it should be incorporated into the diets of vegetarians to avoid problems relating to B12 deficiency such as pernicious anaemia and nerve damage. If I had a dollar for every wilting vegan that could use a good steak ... lucky for them there's a wheatgrass!

As with other sprouted seeds, sprouted wheat berries provide a vitality superior to other foods due to the fact that the crop 'harvest' coincides with consumption, therefore there is no dying off period as with other picked, packed and shipped plant foods. During the sprouting process, the seeds have already been partially pre-digested by the powerful enzymes and rich vitamin content, thus enabling the body to assimilate the valuable nutrients more readily.

An active ingredient of wheatgrass lies in the crude chlorophyll, the green pigment that gives colour to plants and the 'blood' of all plant life. It has a chemical structure almost identical to that of human blood, haemoglobin. Notice the health and thrive of plants when they have enjoyed exposure to Nature's elements - sun, air, soil and water. Once these elements are absorbed they are then synthesised into chlorophyll. Like the chlorophyll found in other dark green leafy vegetables such as spinach and silver beet, the wheatgrass chlorophyll is far more potent due to the immediate ingestion - straight from the organic crop to your system. Extra fresh, extra vitality.

Wheatgrass possesses highly concentrated enzymes such as super oxide dismutase (SOD), a powerful anti-aging antioxidant that can slowdown the effects of potentially carcinogenic molecules and help to neutralise free radical exposure on the cells. SOD acts synergistically with minerals such as zinc and copper within the cells promoting anti-inflammatory activity.

It is thought to reduce the arthritis process, curtail inflammations linked with cardiovascular disease, repair DNA and stimulate cell immunity. Other enzymes found in wheatgrass facilitate digestion by detoxifying internal pollutants from chemically treated food, radiation, drugs and environmental carcinogens. The living enzyme energy of wheatgrass is testament to a healthier you and the potential rejuvenation of the nation.

RECIPES AND REMEDIES FROM AUSTRALIA'S LEADING SPA CHEF

Wheatgrass Beetini

* Yields approximately four shots

60ml wheatgrass juice
4 beets, peeled and juiced juice of 4 beets
1 teaspoon grated ginger

- Cut off 3-4 handfuls of fresh wheatgrass from the tray and extract the juice in a fruit press
- Juice the beets and combine with a little of the pulp so as to thicken the juice. Add ginger to the beetroot juice
- In small shot glasses, pour in the beetroot and ginger juice, then carefully layer the wheatgrass juice on the top. Serve immediately

Image thanks to Lisa Saad Photography

Grains

Grains and legumes are the only food groups that contain all nutrients essential to our health: proteins, carbohydrates, fats, vitamins, minerals and fibre. Most grains are acid forming; therefore excess will create a build up of acid in the body tissues causing such inflammatory arthritic problems. An alkalising balance is therefore required. Vegetables and fruit provide the required alkalising balance.

Annemarie Colbin, founder of The Natural Gourmet Cooking School in New York extols the virtues of selective grain consumption. She states that when her students change their diet from overly refined carbohydrates to wholegrains and cereals, they became more grounded. It was a transition "from a fragmented, alienated, self-centered view to one of connection, integration and oneness" she reckons.

The Immortal Grain
Amaranth (Chenopodium quinoa)

In Greek fable, amaranth was the never fading flower, the emblem of immortality. It also belongs to the goosefoot family, just like rice and it can be used in puddings, or as a sticky porridge. Uncooked amaranth makes a crunchy topping for salads and breads and maybe sprouted for salads.

Amaranth is very high in the amino acid lysine, which is commonly low in most other grains. So this makes it a superfood when combined with other grains because it becomes a complete protein.

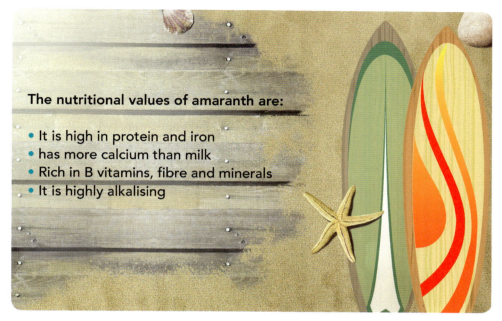

The nutritional values of amaranth are:

- It is high in protein and iron
- has more calcium than milk
- Rich in B vitamins, fibre and minerals
- It is highly alkalising

The Antiquated Grain
Barley *(Hordeum vulgare)*

In the philosophy of Ayurveda, barley represents renewal and abundance. An ancient grain that originated in the East, barley was once more prolific than wheat.

The barley grain is composed of five parts. The pearl is the central part, which is covered by the starchy endosperm layer, then the aleurone layer. The two outer layers are the indigestible hulls.

Pearled barley is the most refined and least nutritious part of the grain. It contains the proteins hordein and gluten (though not as much as wheat). It is most commonly used in soups because its high gluten content is a natural thickening agent and makes an excellent addition to the stuffing for the Christmas turkey.

Hulled barley grain (also known as pot or Scotch barley) has had the hull and part of the bran removed. It is also used in soups and casseroles and has a restoring and nurturing nature.

The Japanese use hulled barley called hato mugi, which has been compressed and enriched. Barley is the most acid forming grain thus it would be advisable to combine it with an alkalising grain such as millet or vegetables. In its whole form it has twice the amount of calcium, three times the iron and more protein than the pearled variety.

Remedies

- The restorative benefits of barley water date back to Hippocrates.
- A herbal tea or tisane of barley water maybe prepared by infusing 1-2 tablespoons of barley per litre of water to treat fever
- Barley water has diuretic and laxative actions, which may alleviate constipation, flatulence and kidney stone pain
- The slightly mucilaginous liquid helps to soothe sore throats and relieve upset stomachs more effectively than ordinary water
- The protease inhibitors in barley grains have cancer preventing suppressing intestinal carcinogens
- Its refreshing emollient properties are useful as a poultice for eczema and other summer heat conditions such as heat rash and sunburn
- Roasted barley tea may be substituted for coffee granules

Against The Grain
Buckwheat - *(Fagopurum esculentum)*

Though not botanically classified as a true grain, buckwheat comes from the common dock and rhubarb family. Buckwheat is actually a fruit kernel. Nevertheless, it is usually categorised as a grain.

It belongs to the goosefoot family (Chenopodiaceae) that includes, spinach, rhubarb, beets and sorrel.

Most people would know the buckwheat flour used in American breakfast pancakes and Russian blinis, however, the lesser known buckwheat noodles are very much a part of Japanese cuisine, especially in the summer when they are served chilled over ice with wasabi and shoyu. Whole roasted buckwheat groats that have had the husk removed are called kasha.

Japanese cuisine is bountiful with a variety of noodles collectively known as menrui. Soba is made mostly from buckwheat flour and its heritage lies within the old ways of Edo, Tokyo's former guise. Further south in Kyoto and Osaka, the Udon - a wheat-based noodle - is prominent in the cooking.

It is customary to make yourself heard when eating noodles - the more slurping the better! Quite the contrast to the silent ceremony observed in eating much of the cuisine.

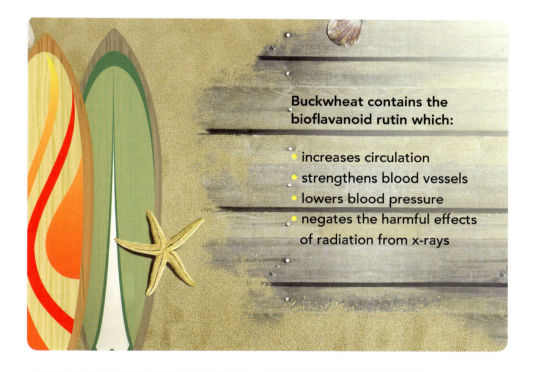

Buckwheat contains the bioflavanoid rutin which:

- increases circulation
- strengthens blood vessels
- lowers blood pressure
- negates the harmful effects of radiation from x-rays

Remedies

- When used in a poultice, buckwheat can treat scalds and burns
- Blend with lotus roots as a tea to aid high blood pressure

Buckwheat With Coconut and Almonds

100 g buckwheat groats
20 g soy grits
20 g lecithin granules
20 g coconut, toasted
20 g natural almonds
500 ml almond milk
Apple juice concentrates or honey to serve

- Heat almond milk very gently, add buckwheat and simmer for 20 minutes until tender
- Add remaining ingredients and top with apple juice concentrate or honey if desired

The American Grain
Corn - *(Zea mais)*

Whereas in Australia wheat is the base grain, corn is the most prolific grain in America and is used from petrol pumps (ethanol) to party pies. Native to Central America, corn was barely used until the end of the 15th century when it would become the most utilised crop on the planet to this day.

> *"Few plants can manufacture quite as much organic matter (and calories) from the same quantities of sunlight and water and basic elements as corn. There are some 45,000 items in the average American supermarket, and more than a quarter of them contain corn. At the same time, the food industry has done a good job of persuading us that the 45,000 different items or SKUs (stock keeping units) represent genuine variety rather than the clever rearrangements of molecules extracted from the same plant."*
> Michael Pollan, What's Eating America, Smithsonian.com

- Corn may be eaten as kernels from the cob, or ground into cornmeal for porridge, cakes, breads or polenta. You cannot buy any processed food in a North American supermarket, which does not contain corn in one form or another
- Corn flour is a gluten free effective thickening agent. It has been used by the Chinese to add body and gloss to their cuisine

- Corn oil and corn syrup are found in most processed foods such as confectionery and salad dressings and more recently have given rise to an overwhelming health debate
- It is an integral part of virtually all processed food including margarine, MSG, condiments, ice cream. It provides body to sauces and soups by stabilising the moisture content, helps food to hold its shape and assists in promoting a long shelf life

So don't be fooled, just because it contains corn certainly does not make a product healthy. The only way to enjoy it for nutritional content is straight from the garden, steamed or roasted.

The Plague of the Polenta Eaters
Polenta

Pellagra is a malnutrition wasting disease that is caused by a dietary deficiency of niacin (vitamin B3). It causes skin lesions and can lead to dementia. Pellagra occurred because the corn mush, which was the only food available to the poor, contained niacin, which, without the amino acid tryptophan, could not be released.

Well aware of this amino acid dilemma, the Native Americans and Mexicans provided some significant early examples of health giving food combining. The Native Americans accompanied their corn meals with beans and also soaked their corn in alkalising solutions of water combined with the ashes of burnt shell and branches. The Mexicans combined their refried beans with corn tortillas. They used lime as a means of releasing the niacin content and this also softened the skin of the kernels making them easier to digest. Thus, the process of food combining has been in full swing for centuries.

Citrus Polenta Pancakes

Yields 10 approximately

½ cup polenta
Pinch Murray River salt
175ml boiling water
1 egg
½ cup milk
30 grams melted butter
1 orange, zest and juice
75 grams gluten free flour
Coconut oil for frying

- Mix together all dry ingredients
- Beat the egg, add in the melted butter and milk
- Fold in the dry ingredients. Mix until just blended. Fold in the orange juice and zest
- Allow to rest for 10 minutes before frying
- Melt some butter or oil in a skillet on medium high. Dollop in about ½ cup of batter
- Wait for the bubbles to appear and begin popping and then flip over the pancake. Cook until browned

Corn's thermal energy is neutral with a sweet flavour. Its silk is highly diuretic and a tea infusion can be prepared for urinary infections and edema. It enhances appetite, which is probably why it is consumed as a first course.

Blue corn is far more nutritious than its paler cousin. It is cooling and contains twice the iron and nearly twenty five percent more protein.

Stone-ground cornmeal is preferable to the industrial methods of grinding, as freshly harvested corn is just as superior to the canned variety. It is interesting to note however that somehow tins of the creamed version crept into the Chinese restaurants in Australia in such dishes as chicken and sweet corn soup.

The Queen of the Grain
Millet
(Panicum milaceum) Broomcorn
(Pennisetum americanum)
Pearl Millet (Setaria italica) Foxtail Millet

Millet has been a staple grain of Northern China since 5000 BC Chinese legend has it that the Emperor Shen Nung, famed for his agricultural skill, "was aided by divine intervention when the heavens rained millet, which he collected and showed his people how to sow and tend." The hot, dry climates of Asia and Africa do not permit wheat and rice to grow therefore millet has become the major food crop of these regions.

The aleurone layer of millet is a single layer of cells, which is rich in minerals, potassium, magnesium and iron and B-complex vitamins.

- Of all the grains, millet is the only one that and has alkalising properties, (quinoa is also alkalising however it is really a seed and not a grain)
- It contains no gluten making it a refreshing, light summer grain
- Millet is used for unleavened breads and as an alternative for other grains in casseroles
- Millet is moistening and cooling, with a sweet-salty flavour
- The aleurone layer of millet is a single layer of cells that are rich in minerals, potassium, magnesium and iron and B-complex vitamins

Benefits

- Anti-fungal properties
- Soothes nausea and morning sickness - as a porridge or congee with ginger
- Clears heat
- Roasted millet can be used in the treatment of diarrhea - half a cup, three times a day

Folklore

Hansel and Gretel scattered behind them a trail of millet in the forest!

Mares Eat Oats
Oats - (Avena sativa)

"Mares eat oats and does eat oats

And little lambs eat ivy"

Milton Drake, Al Hoffman and Jerry Livingston

Like rye, oats also thrive in colder, less hospitable climates and have been the basic diet of both humans and livestock for centuries. The rolled oats that we know best as a breakfast staple have had the husk removed. They are then steamed and rolled flat. The heating process promotes longer life by inhibiting potentially rancid enzymes from producing harmful fatty acids.

The external layer (husk) of oats contains a shapeless alkaloid that can stimulate the excitability of the muscles. No doubt that is what makes horses fast and frisky!

In her book Everyday Cooking, Mrs. Beeton suggests that:

"Oats are rich in flesh forming qualities, heat givers and nourishing properties, yet they are a cheap food and most easily prepared."

Oats have a warming nature and are sweet and slightly bitter. Being high in soluble fibre, oats help bind unwanted bile and sterols and remove them from the digestive tract.

Remedy

Make an oatmeal poultice to relieve itching by soaking oats in water and tying up in a hanky or tea towel. Apply to itch as required. Great for heat rash and eczema.

The Mother Seed
Quinoa *(Chenopodium quinoa)*

Quinoa derives from the Chenopodium or goosefoot family (as does spinach). It is native to the Andean region of South America where it is the principal food of the area. Its leaves are similar to those of both the spinach and amaranth plants. It is known as a pseudo-cereal because it is technically not a grass. The seeds are cultivated for their highly nutritious protein and calcium components - protein reaching 20% and calcium being higher per milligrams than milk.

Quinoa has the highest content of iron, calcium and (good) fat. Hence, quinoa is referred to as the 'mother grain'.

The popularity of an ingredient may be steeped in a plethora of origins – economical, agricultural, seasonal – often it's a social or health trend that is dictated by chefs, the media and consumer demand. Quinoa, an ancient native seed originally from South America is a case of all of the above.

A decade ago this alkalising cereal was just beginning to show her face on less than a handful of Australian menus and would only be found in the dustiest of health food shops. More recently she has been welcomed into the stable of grains and other carbohydrates and billed as the superfood with a royal title. "Queen-o-a" rolls of the tongue of the uninitiated, however the seed is pronounced 'keen-wah' and its culinary highlight of recent years was to be the cover girl for the 2010 September edition of Australian Gourmet Traveller with a variation of a recipe I had been teaching for years.

Published with the permission of Walkley Award Winning cartoonist First Dog on the Moon.
http://www.firstdogonthemoon.com.au/

Sardine Fillets with Minted Quinoa, Currant and Pine Nut Salad

Serves four

16 sardine fillets - preferably West Australian sardines
1 cup quinoa
1 cup water
100 grams currants
100 grams pine nuts
2 lemons zest and juice
1 cup fresh mint leaves washed, dried
2 tablespoons olive oil
Salt and pepper to taste
Extra currants and pine nuts to garnish

- Place quinoa in a large saucepan and cover with water
- Bring to the boil, reduce heat and simmer gently until all the liquid has been absorbed
- When cool, fluff with a fork and add currants, lemon zest and juice, pine nuts, mint and olive oil. Season as desired
- Heat a little oil in a non-stick pan and place sardine fillets, skin side down. Gently pan fry for 4 minutes skin side only
- Spoon small amounts the quinoa salad on to serving plates Carefully place sardines on top.
- Garnish with additional pine nuts and currants, drizzle with olive oil and serve

The Life-Giving Grain
Rice
(Oryza sativa)

*"Eat short grain rice when the days are short
and long grain rice when the days are long."*

Chinese proverb

My mate Ruski - who is a bit Chinese himself and helped to edit this book -reckons that his mum used to say that for every grain of rice you left on your plate you would have a spot on your face. Sweet!

Globally, rice is one the most prolifically consumed cereal grains. Generally thought to be indigenous to China, the humble rice grain is derived from an annual grass that dates back to the fourth-century BC.

Internationally, rice features in most cuisines, each country having definite preferences:

- Short stickier, white oval, translucent rice grains in Japan
- The short grain in Spain (as used when preparing Paella)
- Medium grain in China
- The Chinese also use this grain to produce the 'rice water' called congee
- The long grain delicate white Basmati rice is the only one consumed in Ayurvedic medicine in India simply because it is so easily digested
- The elongated, transparent fragrant Jasmine rice and some short grain rice are preferred in South East Asia. Glutinous short grain rice becomes sticky when cooked, hence it is used in sticky rice pudding.
- The Italians favour the 'grey' rice from aborio when preparing risotto and the Japanese, use short grain rice for Sushi. This is the traditional choice, which is not surprising because they best suit their respective dishes

One of my great loves, German, a Filipino exclaimed in horror when I first confronted him with a bowl of steaming brown rice. For him brown rice was pig fodder!! Incidentally, he also used to joke that risotto was Italian for "who stuffed up the rice"! Actually he uses an expletive that I cannot write here.

Sadly, this is indicative of a lack of awareness that consumption of the complete grain is essential. Why? Because, when rice is milled and polished it loses nutrients such as zinc and thiamine contained within the aleurone layer. Various processes aimed at making rice whiter necessitate the removal of the outer layers of the grain (an important source of minerals and vitamins) and detract considerably from its dietetic value.

The outer layer of rice (and wheat) complements the inner. Zinc in the outer layer is necessary to counter the detrimental effects of the highly toxic micro mineral cadmium. Without zinc from the outer layer, cadmium from the inner layer will go unchecked creating havoc for the cardiovascular, digestive, excretory and immune systems and create all sorts of inflammatory problems for the gut in general such as bloating, flatulence and pain.

Wild rice is not rice as such, it is more closely related to the corn family. It is the staple of North American Indians, who call it "water grass" and it is also rich in B vitamins and has a higher protein content.

The protein rich aleurone layer contains significant amounts of:

- Cancer preventing lignans and phenols
- Its rich supply of B vitamins are supportive of the nervous system as well as being nourishing, detoxifying and strengthening and beneficial in the treatment of indigestion, diarrhoea, vomiting and nausea.
- It contains a rich supply of minerals including: magnesium, potassium, phosphorus, calcium - and zinc

While the properties and energetics of most rice are generally warming with a sweet flavour, Basmati rice is slightly aromatic, more delicate and is more cooling. The finest Basmati is organically grown in the Himalayas, however the Thais have a locally grown variety.

Basmati – King of Rice

The difference between basmati rice and regular rice is how much the rice has been processed. Basmati has a special aroma due to a chemical called 2-acetyl-1-pyrroline, which exists about 12 times more than other rice giving basmati its special scent.

Mahatma Breakfast
Toasted Rolled Rice and Coconut Porridge

Serves 2

This deliciously warming Ayurvedic gluten-free breakfast idea came from our good friends at Mondo Organics in Brisbane. I've tweaked it a little to suit what was in my pantry today. The perfect breaky after Sunday morning yoga and a great way to start your surfing day.

2 cups rolled rice
½ cup shredded or flaked coconut
½ tablespoon coconut oil
2/3 cup dates, finely chopped
2 teaspoons freshly peeled and grated turmeric (½ teaspoon of the dried stuff)
½ tsp ground cardamom
½ tsp ground cinnamon
½ tsp ground ginger
Dash rosewater

To serve

2 teaspoons raw honey
½ green apple, grated or a squeeze of lime
¼ cup biodynamic yoghurt
1 tablespoon roasted pepitas or sunflower seeds

- Place the oil in a large frying pan and add the rice and coconut
- Roast in a non-stick frying pan on a medium heat until starting to change colour
- Add 4 cups of water, dates and spice
- Cook until thick porridge starts to form – about 5 minutes
- Remove from heat and stir in honey
- Serve with grated green apple, yoghurt, roasted seeds and/or a squeeze of lime

Rice Remedies

- A brown rice diet for a few days will assist digestive disorders
- Half a teaspoon of ground rice taken three times daily may be helpful in the treatment of diarrhoea
- A handful of raw brown rice only for breakfast may effectively expel parasites, just be sure to have a cast iron gut and chew well!
- Half a cup of cooked white rice will also help to alleviate symptoms of travel sickness and help to bind "Travellers Diarrhoea" - a handy tip for travellers, especially in Asia
- Make a poultice with cooked rice poultice for burns and scalds
- Brown basmati rice contains about 20% more fibre compared to other types of brown rice

Rye Makes Muscle, Wheat Makes Fat
Rye - *(Secale cereale)*

Rye berries come from a pasture and fodder grass known as rye grass and it is a relatively recent cereal when compared to wheat and barley.

Rye grass is sturdy and can tolerate cold climate conditions better than wheat and was the staple grain of most of Europe until the mid-nineteenth century.

Rye flour has a longer shelf life than wheat. Traditional Germanic loaves prepared from rye flour are black bread (schwartzbrod) and pumpernickel. Rye flour lacks the glutinous proteins that make other dough pliable, thus rye loaves are sturdy, dense and improve in flavour after a few days.

They have a heavy texture with a bittersweet flavour. The bitter flavour lends itself very well to sourdough baking methods. In addition to its hearty taste, rye is particularly high in B group vitamins, potassium, magnesium and is a good source of iron and protein.

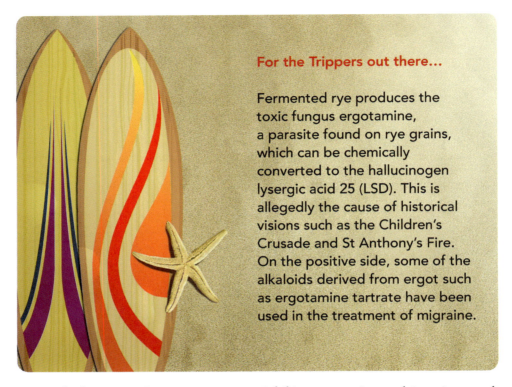

For the Trippers out there…

Fermented rye produces the toxic fungus ergotamine, a parasite found on rye grains, which can be chemically converted to the hallucinogen lysergic acid 25 (LSD). This is allegedly the cause of historical visions such as the Children's Crusade and St Anthony's Fire. On the positive side, some of the alkaloids derived from ergot such as ergotamine tartrate have been used in the treatment of migraine.

- Rye, which contains B vitamins, protease inhibitors, potassium, calcium, is neutral, sweet-bitter and drying
- It increases strength and endurance and therefore alleviates fatigue
- It contributes to the formation of muscle, bone, hair and nails
- Due to its drying absorbent nature, rye can be used to clear liver stagnancy, unclog blood vessels and aid in decreasing body fat
- Rye is also useful in the treatment of anemia and supporting digestion

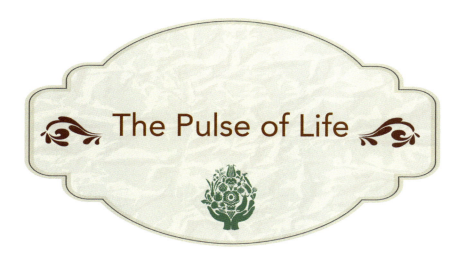

Legumes (Leguminosae)

This botanical family incorporates 'a plant that bears seeds in a pod, which splits open down both seams when ripe.' Dried beans, lentils and chickpeas and are collectively known as legumes or pulses.

The Japanese Bean
Adzuki Beans

These small reddish-brown beans are my favourite. They are a staple of Japanese cuisine and hold the key to many digestive problems of the Western world. The Chinese use them for drying damp conditions such as thrush, Candida and to clear phlegm – all which are prevalent in our society. Damp conditions traditionally reflect the intake of too much greasy food and a sedentary lifestyle - in short an imbalance - yet they can also represent an internal yeast overgrowth such as Candida or edema.

Most of who attempt the painstaking task of shedding kilos will know how frustrating it is after cutting down on fat and increasing cardiovascular activity that nothing diminishes - a soul destroying realisation. However, not all is yet lost. Once you acquire an early affinity for the energetics of food, you will begin to comprehend their healing properties.

This is demonstrated with the adzuki. First, soak the beans overnight, drain, refresh, cover with water and simmer. Note that the cooking water starts to evaporate very quickly - and if you were to leave the kitchen you may come back to a black mess in your saucepan. Believe me, I know! Add more water while they simmer. Now start to appreciate why the water is disappearing so fast -it is not just because it is boiling; it is because the adzuki beans are absorbing the liquid, i.e. they are drying out the pot.

So, consider the effect that they will have on the body if this is what happens to them during the cooking process. They will potentially dry out unused bodily fluid and absorb and eliminate it. Surely this has potential and if the person has a cold and damp condition, then those warming and drying foods are combined to remedy their plight.

The Hippy Bean
Mung Beans

Mung beans are tiny olive green (or black) beans originating in India and are known principally grown here in Australia, as well as Thailand and China.

Like adzuki, mung beans are also cooling in their thermal nature. They are most commonly known for their sprouting potential, yet mung beans can be prepared in a similar way to adzuki beans.

With such an association with Woodstock and all things hippy, the mung bean may have turned and bolted by now - thank goodness it still abounds, for mung beans are vital - in fact, they are the business when it comes to cell regeneration.

They are detoxifying and support liver function. Energetically, they are contractive which can help to bring about balance after the effects of too much expansive food and stimulants.

They have a sweet flavour and a very cooling, making them an ideal foodstuff for the summer and those who suffer from damp heat conditions. Like adzuki, they are also very drying and can be used in the treatment of food and drug poisoning and can to counteract the effects of alcohol.

The Mung & The Stressless

While the mere mention of a Mung bean usually conjures up images of a peace, love and the lentil lifestyle, the history of the mung bean transcends way back to the antique diets of the East. Certainly, these spheres of jade did enjoy celebrity status during the 70s by providing a vehicle for many a hippie feast, but this was only testament to what the ancient healing cultures already knew about their abilities.

The Ayurvedic principles laid down by the Maharishi Ayurveda celebrate a holistic approach to health and consider the mung bean to be the most nourishing and digestible of all legumes. In Indian cuisine, mung beans are coupled with fragrant warming spices such as cumin and coriander seeds, which increase their thermal energy and enhance their subtle flavour.

Traditional Chinese medicine states the healing properties of the mung bean to be highly detoxifying and cleansing. The Chinese revere them even more for their medicinal prowess than their culinary capacity, especially in decreasing the levels of triglycerides from the blood, thus providing support for the body's cardiovascular system and reduction of overall toxicity.

Mung beans have a cooling property when digested properly. They help to lower the temperature of our internal systems and are therefore beneficial for people who suffer from heat conditions such as sunburn, high blood pressure and eczema. They are best enjoyed as sprouts during the summer months to keep the body cool. It is also worth noting that consumption of the cooking juices from simmered beans can alleviate the effects of food poisoning.

Therapeutic Notes

As a member of the legume family, they can be very easily sprouted, yielding a crop ready to enjoy within a day or two. Like all other sprouted foods, the thriving nutrient value continues after harvest. The simple germination process can increase the vitamin C content by up to 600 times, supplying nearly half the recommended dietary intake in just one serving. Rich in protein and the sulphur containing amino acid methionine - which works as an antioxidant - they can prevent excessive fat build-up in the liver and have an overall calming effect on the body. Just a cup of mung bean sprouts per day will provide the body with approximately 1 gram of vitamin B17, the recommended daily dose.

Vitamin B17, also known as Laetrile and Amygdaline, is a contentious vitamin that is also found in the kernels of stone fruit, especially apricots. B17 contains one- cyanide with two-sugars and one-benzaldehyde molecules, forming a nitriloside compound. It is the molecule of cyanide that has attracted controversy due to its use in cancer therapy and certain authorities argue its validity sighting possible cyanide toxicity. Nevertheless, there seems to be strong evidence suggesting its healing potential.

Cancer cells, however, release the enzyme, ß-glucosidase which catalyses the release of the cyanide and then poisons the cancer cells. The jury is still out on the merit of this vitamin and its use in the treatment of cancer. It has been banned in the US, yet there is much evidence pointing in its favour and numerous healing clinics have been established in neighbouring areas such as Tijuana, Mexico, with very encouraging results.

Forever Mung - Minted Mung Beans with Ginger

200 gram biodynamic dried mung beans soaked
   for 4 hours or overnight
1 tablespoon cold pressed, great quality vegetable oil
4 shallots, peeled, finely minced
3 cloves garlic, finely minced
2 tablespoons fresh ginger, finely minced
½ teaspoon Szechuan peppercorns (or black), cracked
6 Kaffir lime leaves, stems removed, finely sliced
1 cup Vietnamese mint, washed, dried and finely minced
500 ml good vegetable stock

- Drain soaked mung beans, rinse and set aside. Heat oil in a deep, heavy based pot. Add shallots, garlic and ginger and lightly fry until most of the oil has been absorbed
- Continue to cook gently until the some of the oil has been released - about 3 minutes. Add the peppercorns, lime leaves and mint and combine well. Add the drained mung beans and sauté for a moment and then add the stock
- Allow to simmer gently for about 45 minutes (pending on soaking time), until the stock has been absorbed and the beans are tender. Adjust seasoning if required
- Serve alone or with a spoonful of tofu and mung bean whip

A census taker once tried to test me.
I ate his liver with some fava beans and nice Chianti.

Hannibal Lecter – The Silence of the Lambs

The Hannibal Bean
Fava, Baba (broad, horse, field) Beans

Fava beans were allegedly the original bean cultivated in Europe. They are at their most delicious when eaten fresh. The dried variety is adequate, but nowhere near the flavour and texture of the green.

Broad beans arrive in flat pods and when unzipped, expose a green bean about the size of a ten-cent piece. The pods are usually discarded, however maybe eaten if young enough.

The beans should be cooked to remove any potential toxic reactions, a condition called Fauvism, which is an acute type of anemia that results from an enzyme deficiency in the red blood cells.

The Mexican Bean
Red Kidney Beans

"Red Beans and rice I could eat a place twice.
Well yes most people on the planet eat beans and rice.
They can't afford beef or they think cows are nice."

Michael Franti

Probably the best known pulse, kidney beans are a major ingredient of traditional Mexican food. Their availability dates back to Prehistoric times. They have a cooling thermal nature with a sweet taste and may be used diuretically in the treatment of edema (fluid retention) and to reduce swellings. These beans are high in fibre and possess sizable amounts of magnesium and calcium.

The Butter Bean
Lima Beans

Sometimes known as butter beans, these creamy-white coloured flat beans resemble fava beans in shape and have high levels of both sodium and potassium. When cooked they have a floury texture due to their high starch levels their skins may separate during cooking. Lima beans are highly alkalizing which can help balance ailments such as arthritis, headaches, eczema, conjunctivitis, low energy, frequent infections that are aggravated by too much acid-forming food in the diet.

The Peace Pulse
Lentils

Another ancient legume, lentils have their origins in the Middle East and boast more than fifty variations. They do not usually require pre-soaking and so can be prepared quickly, but they should be rinsed well then cooked in plenty of water as they also surprisingly 'thirsty' little pulses.

Most common varieties include brown, which retain the skin and red, without skins, or the smaller French Le Puy lentil. Lentils stimulate the adrenal system, support the heart, encourage circulation and are a good kidney tonic.

The Beauty Bean
Haricot Beans

Known as Navy, Boston and Northern beans, these are small white beans made famous by Mr. Heinz. They have a cooling nature with a sweet flavour and they are said to 'promote beautiful skin' says Paul Pitchford, author of Healing with Whole Foods whom I certified with in 2010.

The Middle Eastern Pea
Chickpeas - *(Cicer arietinum)*

Also know as garbanzos and channa, chickpeas claim to fame is that they are the main ingredient in hummus. Being very rich in iron, vitamin A, C and folic acid (B9), they are also higher in fat than most other pulses, except soybeans, which are the highest. They are also high in pangamic acid (vitamin B15), which encourages stamina and strength. They are therefore suitable in weight training to build muscle mass. Chickpeas have a sweet flavour and are beneficial to the heart.

The Lucky Pea
Black-Eyed Peas *(Vigna unguiculata)*

As the signature legume of the southern food in the United States for over 300 years, black-eyed peas are said to bring luck in the New Year and are therefore traditionally eaten on New Year's Eve.

Originating in Africa, they are sometimes referred to as cow peas or black-eyed beans and are high in vitamin B9 or Folic acid - essential in pregnancy for the prevention of neural tube defects such as, Spina bifida and Anencephaly, where babies are born with a congenital absence of all or part of the brain. As the oral contraceptive pill lowers Folic acid, it is important to have adequate intake before conception.

Black-eyed peas can be sprouted and are suitable for soups and stews.

Preparation & Cooking

To soak: Most dried beans need to be soaked overnight in plenty of cold water. Mung beans and lentils can be soaked for minimum of an hour or so. Italian, Greek and Middle Eastern cooks soak broad beans for up to 48 hours with frequent changes of water and then pop the beans out of the very tough skins. Dried broad beans are often sold already skinned. Discard any beans that are discoloured or that float to the top when the soaking water and bean are agitated. Always discard the soaking water as it contains phytic acid that binds with all legumes often creating gas and wind in the digestion.

Quick Method: If you have forgotten to soak them overnight, pour boiling water over them and leave for 3 hours. Discard this water and continue as if the beans have been soaked overnight.

To Cook: Cover the soaked beans generously with fresh cold water and bring to a boil. Simmer gently for (see time chart below) or until the beans are tender (test by tasting them). Avoid stirring the beans, as they tend to break up and do not salt the cooking water as this toughens the skins, causing the bean to split.

Type of Bean	Amount	Instructions	Cooking time	Approx Yield	Comments
Aduki	1 c. dried	Overnight soak	30 – 45′	3 cups	
Black Beans	1 c. dried	Overnight soak	55 – 60′	2 ¼ cups	Colour fades, cook with lid slightly agar to avoid boilovers.
Chick-peas	1 c. dried	Overnight soak. Discard water after first boil. Use fresh tepid water and proceed	Approx 1 hour	2 cups	Very foamy. Needs skimming.
Broad-beans (large, split peeled)	1 c. dried		15 – 20′	1 2/3 cups	Very soft, Does not hold its shape. Good for purees.
Broad –beans (large, whole dried)	1 c. dried		35 – 40′	2 cups	After soaking, outer skins pull off easily. Some beans split open, some disintegrate to thicken sauce while cooking.
Green & yellow split peas	1 c. dried	Do not soak	45 – 60′	2 cups	For purees or soups and stews. Disintegrates.
Green Lentils	1 c. dried	Do not soak	Salad: 20 – 25′ Main: 30 – 40′ Soups: 60′	2 ¼ cups	Full of flavour
Brown Lentils	1 c. dried	Do not soak	Salad: 15 –20′ Main: 25 – 35′ Soups: 60′	2 ½ cups	A bit more defined, earthy taste than green lentils.
Whole Red Lentils	1 c. dried	Do not soak	Salad: 6 – 8′ Main: 10′ Soups: 20′	2 ¼ cups	Pungent, turns golden when cooked. Will keep shape if salt or acid are added immediately after cooking.
Red Kidney Beans	1 c. dried		45 – 60′		Foams up easily. Very tender. Cook with lid ajar to avoid boil-over.

Talking Turkey

Serotonin is one of our good-mood neurotransmitters – derived from melatonin that is found extensively in the gut – and is secreted through the gastrointestinal tract - up to 80%. It modulates perception, cognition mood, emotion, sleep and appetite. It needs a few essential nutrients to activate it and one of those is the amino acid called tryptophan that helps the body produce the B vitamin niacin. Tryptophan helps the body relax and also induces sleep. It is prevalent in a number of foods, especially warm milk - which is why we are often fed that as kids – and turkey. Think about the Christmas day feast in Australia and the de rigueur snooze required afterwards and you'll understand the tryptophan effect.

Salad of turkey, berries, nuts with local sprouts, micro herbs

Salad of Turkey, Berries, Nuts with Local Sprouts, Micro Herbs

Serves two as an entrée or four as a side

Here's a fancy festive salad to make the most of leftovers from Christmas day or as a beautifully healthy alternative to the traditional roast bird.

This recipe will work well with berries, cherries, nectarine or mango. The turkey I prefer is grown by my dear friends at Green Ag in the Darling Downs in South East Queensland. Thye turkeys are grown in small groups and the growers pay attention to their care and diet with their unique organic GreenAg feed blend - as well as playing them baroque music to keep the birds calm and happy! Oh to be a Green Ag bird!

For the salad
1 cup cooked turkey meat, skin off, shredded
1 cup assorted sprouts – fresh from the Farmers' Market
1 cup nuts such as almonds and/or pecans, halved lengthways
Assorted micro herbs such as red garnet, chard, red radish and sorrel

Very Berry Dressing
1 cup fresh berries, roughly chopped
4 tablespoons macadamia oil
1 tablespoon white balsamic or raspberry vinegar
1 lime, juice only
Cracked black pepper

- Shred turkey finely and combine with sprouts and nuts
- Whisk dressing ingredients together well and gently toss through the salad
- Garnish generously with freshly snipped micro herbs

The Pineal Gland – The Glad Eye

The pineal gland has long been regarded as the location of the Third Eye and even has its own rods and cones and interior retina and is thought to be a natural hyper-gate or trans-dimensional access point throughout the ages. The 'third eye' is considered by Indian mystics as our antenna or junction pint where energy all energy comes together.

The ineal gland is a pea-sized conical endocrine gland attached to the roof of the third ventricle of the brain. It is shaped like a pinecone and a pine nut, hence the name but more importantly it governs the modulation of melatonin.

Melatonin is light sensitive so when a room is completely dark there is a greater increase of the production of the melatonin, which in turn helps to encourage sleep. Diminished levels of melatonin may be linked to episodes of jet lag and sleep disorders.

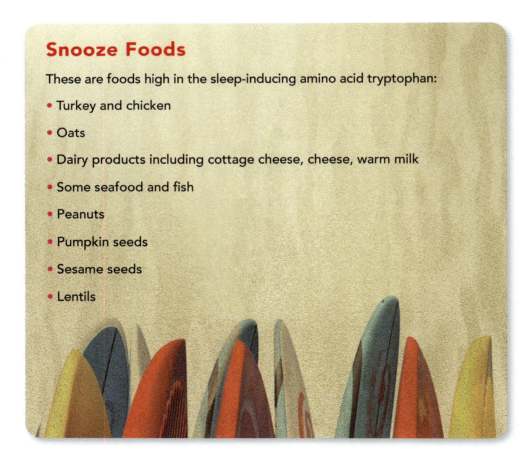

Snooze Foods

These are foods high in the sleep-inducing amino acid tryptophan:

- Turkey and chicken
- Oats
- Dairy products including cottage cheese, cheese, warm milk
- Some seafood and fish
- Peanuts
- Pumpkin seeds
- Sesame seeds
- Lentils

Seared Lime Tofu with Crunchy Shoots, Nuts & Leaves

Serves four

200 grams firm tofu, sliced into 2cm x 1 cm
1 tablespoon lime olive oil
100 grams rocket washed, dried
50 grams assorted bean sprouts - mung, snow pea shoots
¼ Spanish onion, very finely sliced
1 stalk celery, finely sliced 5cm batons
2 tablespoons raw almonds, skin on, roughly chopped
2 tablespoons pepitas (pumpkin seeds)

Dressing
2 tablespoons lime olive oil
I dessertspoon mirin (Japanese rice wine)
½ lime, zest and juice
½ teaspoon grated ginger

- Heat the tablespoon oil in a skillet and light sear tofu slices for 2 minutes either side
- Whisk dressing ingredients together
- Then add rocket leaves, sprouts, onion, celery, nuts and seeds
- Add seared tofu and combine gently
- Drizzle with a thread of olive oil to serve

Gland All Over

The 21st Century has brought with it remarkable research into health and the healing process. Contrarily, stress-related illnesses are rapidly increasing across the globe. Multiple episodes of negative stress reactions have a direct link to depleted states of health including Chronic Fatigue Syndrome (CFS), mood change, depression, insomnia, stomach disorders, Irritable Bowel Syndrome, food sensitivities and can cause well-documented dramatic changes to our blood pressure and heart rate.

Stress has become the "Band-Aid Banner" for many of our problems, particularly in the work place. How often do we refer to our 'stressful lives', or being 'really stressed' at work, without actually identifying the cause? While we may lay blame on the boss, our colleagues and deadlines, how often do we actually look further to establish why we are responding in this way? It is imperative to remember that stress is predominantly our emotional reaction to a difficult situation that may then manifest in the physical body as a sign or symptom of poor health.

The stress phenomenon is not specific; it is an all-encompassing umbrella complex that reaches out to every demographic. Stress can be triggered by an emotional, environmental or physical response to vast array of stressors in modern life.

How stress depletes the body of its vital resources is a complex and intricate mechanism. Typically, the "Neurea-transit" and hormonal highways are tested to their limits, as they react with their daily "fight or flight" responses. The bulk of this energy is derived from the Adrenal glands, which nestle snugly upon each kidney and produce the hormone Adrenaline. A constant stress reaction will ultimately see a decline in the amount of readily available adrenaline, thus resulting in the debilitating energy burnout such as Chronic Fatigue Syndrome.

To put things into perspective: When it comes to stress and busy lives, contemplate this: as soon as your state-of-the-art computer, car, mobile phone or home entertainment system crashes and burns, do you continue to run it into the ground beyond repair? Alternatively, do you panic and seek the immediate help of a professional technician who can fix the problems you know are beyond your capacity? If this is the case, then why would you let your own highly evolved bio-computer, your brain and body, spin down into burnout, doing potentially permanent damage to your personal hard drive?

The Cortisol Connection

In the era of the quick fix and out sourcing our dilemmas to experts, perhaps it is time to embrace a little on-site repair and rebuilding at head office. Truly, it is a labour of love that takes time and cannot be hurried, for it has taken a lifetime for the body to degenerate into that stressed and short-fused state that most of us know and neglect. Remember that there is a self-healing expert in all of us just waiting to get out and live!

Clarity of brain function and unlimited energy stores are tools that we all yearn for in the high-octane business world and personal lives. We expect a good performance from our employees and desire to be healthy and energetic in our own bodies, yet we continue to camouflage our true E (energy) potential with the usual synthetic boosters: coffee, alcohol, processed foods, which result in disrupted sleep patterns and big energy swings. Nothing sets you up better for a highly effective day than a sound night's sleep, a healthy intake of quality, unprocessed, foods and the utilisation of our own energy resources rather than those provided by the faux-caffeine society that we are accustomed to turning to when we feel tired.

The hormone cortisol is produced in the adrenal cortex in response to adrenal cortical stimulating hormone (ACTH) produced in the pituitary gland. Cortisol plays an important role in regulating blood sugar, energy production, inflammation, the immune system and healing.

If you have too little cortisol, you may suffer from fatigue, chronic fatigue, exhaustion and a disease of the endocrine system called Addison's disease. If your adrenal glands are producing too much cortisol, you may develop conditions such as weight gain, especially around the abdomen, depressed immune function with all of the consequences, accelerated aging and stomach ulcers.

Cortisol and Stress

Cortisol is elevated in response to stress. The adrenal glands are not particular, any kind of stress will do. Your stress reaction may be physical, environmental, chemical or imaginary and your primal hard drive is hard wired with automatic responses to protect you from harm, hazard and danger.

While the B vitamins (B3 Niacin, B1 Thiamin, B2 Riboflavin, B6, biotin, pantothenic acid, B12, folic acid) are our defence against stress - by soothing the nervous system, creating pathways to the key chemical messengers we call neurotransmitters - it is the antioxidants that are even more vital for smooth biomechanical and emotional peace.

During the stress response, many things occur. Firstly, the adrenal glands enlarge and begin to secret large doses of the hormones adrenaline and cortisol (adrenal cortical hormones).

When this happens the usual inflammatory responses are suppressed and the body becomes constantly 'on guard' ready for the attack. This is well-documented biochemical reaction known as the Fight or Flight response.

Physiological stress affects the function of the gut by decreasing the all important gut flora lactobacilli and bifidobacteria (see The Yeast Beast).

Stress also increases the risk of:

- Obesity
- Insomnia
- Digestive complaints
- Heart disease
- Depression
- Cold/flu

Is your gut far too busy dealing with your stress to even thinking about burning fat?

When it comes to the frustrating battle of weight maintenance and the stress alarm bells go off, blood sugar levels elevate. Then the glycogen stores in the liver and muscle tissue mobilise which inhibits the digestive function, causing a thinning of the stomach lining and a fast track to ulceration – the classic inflammatory response!

Garlic
The Stinking Rose

*"The honest flavour of fresh garlic is something
I can never have enough of."*

James Beard

Garlic is thought to be native to central Asia and is used prolifically throughout the culinary world. Its history dates back over 5000 years to the ancient world and has always been revered for its medicinal actions by the Chinese. The pungency of the bulb varies from the mild Elephant or Russian garlic, to the stronger common white knobs.

These pungent bulbs are members of the same family as the lily flower. Garlic, leeks, onions, shallots and chives all marry well together or can be an independent flavour and enhancement to any dish. When these aromatic vegetables are combined with chilli and ginger, they provide the foundations for much of the cuisine of South East Asia.

The healing properties of the allilium species are well documented throughout history. Both East and West have embraced them for their culinary value and medical efficacy. Studies of garlic as a healing herb are profound and there is conclusive evidence of garlic lowering the risk of: heart disease, gastric, colon cancer and potentially hazardous cholesterol levels. Although celebrated for their healing effects it is wise to note that they are also powerful herbs and are medicinal thus they need to be used cautiously within the daily diet.

The active healing ingredient in garlic comes from its high anti-oxidative sulphuric compounds, which enter the bloodstream after digestion and are then released through the pores. When garlic cloves are cut the antibacterial agent, allicin is activated. Allicin has the power to: block carcinogens in food, inhibit blood cells from clotting and prevent hardening of the arteries. Its antibacterial properties assist in the fight against internal germ warfare combating bacteria such as E. coli.

Garlic is also an antibiotic. It was in extensive use during the Second World War when doctors prevented gangrene and the toxic poisoning by applying a topical poultice of mashed garlic to the wound.

"No cook who has attained mastery over her craft ever apologises for the presence of garlic in her productions."

Ruth Gottfried, The Questing Cook in Food Lovers' Companion

Unfortunately, thermal processing of garlic inhibits its health benefits so daily consumption of raw garlic is recommended. This need not mean chewing a clove each morning - a very anti-social practice. Raw garlic can be sliced paper thin and added to salads and steamed vegetables, just before serving. There are many garlic supplements available on the market, but why waste precious dollars for a manufactured tablet when the real thing is so abundantly available?

The Dracula Factor

The classic macabre tale of the sinister life of a Romanian Prince known as Dracula has tormented us for over 100 years. An interesting theory regarding vampires is that they suffer from a rare disease known as Porphyria. Symptoms of this illness may include sensitivity to sunlight and only venture out at night. In the most severe form, which is very rare, the sufferers' teeth and bones become fluorescent - shining pink or red. They might actually look horrific." The pale and pasty complexion results from blood not being delivered to the red blood cells, allegedly giving the victim a yearning for blood.

King George III was also said to have suffered from Porphyria, which poisons the immune system and can lead to mental disturbance. The smell of garlic can also nauseate Porphyria patients and worsen their condition. My advice is to always remember to pierce the cloves to release the sulphur compounds before a embarking on a Transylvanian encounter!

Whatever your bite, there is no doubt that garlic is an imperative addition to our daily diet.

Canine Warning

Dogs will tolerate and benefit from garlic whereas onions have a detrimental effect on their digestive tract and must never be given to our canine friends as they may develop haemolytic anaemia causing an abnormal breakdown of red blood cells in the blood vessels or elsewhere in the body.
Be careful never to leave out pizza, take away food, unprotected leftovers on benches and onion residue on your barbeque.

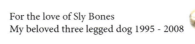

For the love of Sly Bones
My beloved three legged dog 1995 - 2008

Garlic tips

Garlic (and onions) is a natural antibiotic, reducing the incidence of common colds. Combining garlic with the dried pepper from the cayenne chilli will induce a sweating reaction if taken at the onset of the cold.

Garlic is warming and helps to move energy throughout the body. A garlic poultice applied topically to the inflamed area may help to alleviate arthritic pain.

Onions Allilium cepa

The onion family possesses very high quantities of sulphuric compounds (allylic sulphides), which assist in flushing out toxic waste and heavy metal deposits and the metabolism of amino acids.

Dry Onions

These onions may be left in a dry place for a few weeks. Their skins should remain intact, slightly crisp to touch and without dark marks or soft spots.

Shallots, Eschallots

In Australia and parts of Asia, we call small dry brown onions shallots. These milder onions are an essential ingredient in Asian 'rempah' curry pastes.

Red Onions

Also called Spanish onions, these pretty varieties come in different shapes from robust and round to small oval footballs. They have a sweet flavour, which lends itself nicely when finely sliced to a salad of orange segments.

White & Brown Onions

Used in most kitchens as the foundation of many a dish, they will begin to shoot a green stem if forgotten. The white variety is much stronger - and elicits more tears.

Green Onions (Spring Onions - Australia)

These onions are a welcome addition to any salad or stir-fry, however some confusion surrounds them. In Australia, we know these shoots as 'spring onions' or 'scallions' but they are commonly known as shallots in the United States.

Scallions, Spring Onions

Spring onions are cylindrical and approximately the same width at each end.
Tea produced from spring onions is thought to soothe the sharp pain incurred from arthritis.

Salad Onions

Salad onions bulbs are round and larger than those of the Spring onions are. Confused?

Leeks Allium porrum

Leeks are the sweetest of the onion family and are very much a part of French cuisine.

Chives

Chives are the smallest perennial herb belonging to the onion family.

Ginger
The Jewels of the Underground

If spice were to be a crown, then ginger would surely be its golden jewel. Native to Asia, the ginger plant (Zingiber officinale) was one of the earliest commodities to be introduced to European colonies from the East Indies by the Spanish, consequently laying down the foundations of The Spice Trade.

Once the Spaniards delivered this amber spice to the West, the Americas soon naturalised crops, cultivating it enthusiastically and importing some 22,053 cwt. into Europe in 1547. It was so popular that it soon became standard ration amongst George Washington's troops during the Revolutionary War. The West Indies now boasts some of the finest crops, harvesting a shorter, more pungent tan rhizome.

Hailed as "the universal medicine" by Ayurvedic wisdom, the yogis of ancient India were its first enthusiasts, praising the spice for the mental clarity and sweetness of breathe it gave them, which was sure to please their Gods. The name ginger is derived from a Sanskrit word for "horn root". Soon the Chinese embraced it and their interpretations and gave rise to its healing notoriety.

A perennial crop belonging to the botanical family of underground stems called Tuberous Rhizomes; ginger shares its roots with other important spice such as turmeric and galangal (Thai ginger). No Asian dish would be complete without the inclusion of this aromatic spice.

Back in the 70s, fresh ginger was as rare as hens' teeth to find, so as a child, I only knew of the dried spice that lent its flavour to gingerbread men, crystallised ginger and the ginger nut biscuits my father was fond of. Fortunately, the fresh variety is abundant in our shops and markets, thanks to the influx of Asian grocers and restaurants, finally making the supply proportional to the demand.

Its flexibility in the kitchen is paramount as it lends its unique flavour to an atlas of taste, particularly those of the exotic East - whether that be the Far, Middle or South.

Only fresh ginger appears on the Japanese table, never dried. Hajikami "blushing ginger", are long piquant pink shoots that usually accompany grilled dishes, while sweet pickled ginger Beni-shoga, is the garnish always served with sushi. In Burma, an after meal digestive aid called Gin Thoke comprises lemon marinated sliced ginger which turns it pink, then sautéed garlic and toasted seeds.

When buying fresh 'baby' ginger for cooking always look for young 'hands' that are pale yellow gold and have a hint of moisture. Very young ginger has an almost transparent coat with roots tipped with pink. Fresh ginger is fragrant with a light yellow, fibrous interior. It has a fresh hot taste with sharpness likened to that of chilli. Chinese cuisine celebrates ginger for these warming properties, using it to stimulate the appetite and promote digestion by kindling the digestive fire, making it the perfect ingredient for winter.

The older the ginger, the more knotted the knobs and thicker the skin, which requires very fine peeling. The most flavour is derived from the mature root stock therefore if too much peel is removed, essential oils and rich resins may be lost. With young ginger, however, the skin is so fine that is really not worth the trouble, so slice or grate with the skin intact. Young ginger root should be at least one year old before consumption.

Gingerly - with soft steps:
with extreme wariness and delicate gentleness

Medicinally, ginger is a diaphoretic (promotes sweating) and is highly beneficial in treating coughs and colds by clearing phlegm or mucous build up in lungs, sinus and throat. Freshly squeezed ginger juice will help to allay nausea and vomiting symptoms associated with motion and morning sickness and the effects of food poisoning. Ginger may also be used to neutralise strong odours from seafood and less than fresh meats. and as an antidote for seafood poisoning by counteracting the toxic effects – one of its earliest medicinal tasks.

Continuing research suggests that ginger may help to lower cholesterol and reduce the risk of cardiovascular disease by inhibiting platelet aggregation - a contributing factor in atherosclerosis - and the accumulation of plaque within the coronary arteries that can lead to a reduction of blood flow to the cardiac muscle.

RECIPES AND REMEDIES FROM AUSTRALIA'S LEADING SPA CHEF

A Gingerly Paste for Winter

2 pieces peeled fresh ginger, about 1 inch thick
1 bunch fresh coriander, washed and dried
1 fresh red chilli, seeds removed, chopped roughly
4 cloves garlic
Juice and zest of 1 lime
½ teaspoons toasted cumin seeds
½ teaspoon toasted coriander seeds
½ teaspoon turmeric
½ teaspoon sea salt
½ cup olive oil

- Place all ingredients in a food processor and combine until a smooth paste is formed. Use as a base for curries or as a marinade for any fish or meat

Whole Fish With Tamari and Ginger

1 x 750 kg whole bream or snapper
2 tablespoons macadamia nut oil
1 teaspoon freshly grated ginger
8 spring onions, finely chopped
2 teaspoons sesame oil
2 tablespoons tamari
½ bunch fresh coriander, washed and dried

- Scale, clean and wash fish. Steam over boiling water for 15 minutes until cooked through – set aside, keep warm
- Heat macadamia oil and sauté ginger and spring onions until soft but not brown. Remove from heat add sesame oil and tamari
- Remove fish from steamer and place on a serving platter. Place fish on a large serving platter and spoon over the sauce and garnish with chopped coriander

Image by Anson Smart

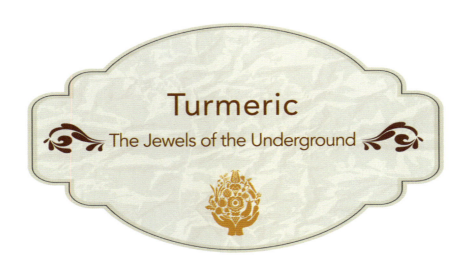

Turmeric
The Jewels of the Underground

Curcumin

Turmeric (Curcuma longa) is a perennial crop belonging to the botanical family of underground stems or spice roots called tuberous rhizomes that also includes ginger and galangal (Thai ginger). The plant is native to South East Asia and also the West Indies. Turmeric is a root plant with fleshy extended stems that run just under the ground and produce shoots and roots for new plants.

A handsome plant that can grow up to five or six feet with a large yellow and white flower spike surrounded by long leaves. Its potent healing properties include the powerful antioxidant called curcumin that gives this Indian spice its characteristic yellow colour to rice and curry dishes. With smaller shoots or fingers than ginger, it has an earthy, slightly bitter flavour with a crisp aromatic nose and a pale to deep yellow flesh inside tan or dark brown skin.

Turmeric is an important spice in Ayurveda – the traditional medicine of India. It can be consumed by all the body types or doshas. Not to be sautéed in oil as the spice is sensitive to long cooking periods so sprinkle over slow-cooking vegetable dishes. The Balinese make a tonic called Jamu consisting of fresh or dried turmeric, lime juice and honey. Jamu is usually found in powder form to which water is usually added and the tonic is steeped before consumption.

Hustle, Bustle & Muscle

Degenerative joint diseases such as Osteoarthritis (rheumatism), typically target specific areas of the body like the hips, knees, fingers, big toes and the spine. Characterised by deep, aching pain with stiffness, Osteoarthritis is usually caused by inflammation of the muscles, ligaments, tendons, or bone that surround the damaged cartilage. Most cartilage degeneration is due to a lack of proteoglycan (chondroitin sulphate), a protein sugar also known as mucopolysaccharides (MPs), which provide the cartilage with the tensile strength required to carry out its supporting role.

Mucopolysaccharides are gel-like substances found naturally within our cartilage that function as shock absorbers. They are special sugars interlaced with amino acids, thus they are protein-rich tissue that enable the joint to perform its elastic and flexible actions. Once deterioration occurs, the area may lead to further wear and tear if not properly treated, causing additional pain and discomfort. An increase of foods rich in protein sugars, such as mucopolysacharrides and glucosamine can encourage the restoration of the joint and tissue repair, essential for healthy joints.

Not only does the dense fibrous collagen/proteoglycan matrix provide cushioning, it also serves as an aqueduct for lubricating substances such as the synovial fluid, found abundantly within the synovial joints. The function of synovial joints is that they are freely movable and their fluid reduces friction by supplying the area with a rich source of nutrients, vital for tissue integrity and maintenance. As joint movement increases, the viscous, clear, pale yellow, gel-like fluid becomes more viscous. Warming up before training stimulates the production and secretion of synovial fluid.

The degradation of proteoglycan reduces the efficiency of the structural function intended to support the freely moving joints. Foods rich in mucopolysacharrides may be of some benefit by strengthening connective tissue, making it more elastic and resilient to stress. They also contain strong anti-inflammatory properties, making them important for the active and elderly. They have enjoyed success when used to reinforce the fibres of cardiac muscle and to protect the vascular system by lowering fat.

The healing properties of MPs treat other inflammatory conditions such as headaches, bursitis, ulcers, respiratory disease, angina and allergies. Protein sugars like glucosamine sulphate stimulate the biosynthesis and the formation of proteoglycans found in the structural matrix of joints. Therefore, nutritional supplementation, preferably through whole food, acts as an agent to slowly reduce inflammation, thus reducing the need for non-steroidal anti- inflammatory drugs (NSAIDs).

Whole foods that deliver the aforementioned anti-inflammatory actions include: the New Zealand Green Lipped Mussel (perna canaliculus), which is widely imported into Australia), shark fins, oats, tripe and onions - the latter being a most unpalatable combination to many! The more popular foods- mussels and oats - are both highly nutritious, simple to prepare and relatively cheap when compared to the cost of NSAIDs.

Mussels (phylum mollusca) are found in most of the world's oceans. Categorically, they belong to the mollusc species that also includes other animals that have a shell, such as: oysters, clams, periwinkles and the octopus, which produces a shell to protect its eggs. Known as bivalves, these opalescent castanets have global culinary foundations, but are probably best loved when prepared in the Mediterranean style - steamed with tomato, garlic and herbs. Interestingly, the Spanish grow one thousand times more pounds of mussel "meat" than the Americans farm cattle for beef and according to a US Department of Agriculture Handbook, the protein content aligns with that of beef. Mussels yield only 25% of the calorie content of beef with approximately 3.3 grams of carbohydrate.

Mussels are indiscriminate filter feeders that pump in excess of 40 litres of water through their bodies to source essential nutrients and oxygen. Their lifespan is anywhere from 10 to 100 years depending on their environment. Adult mussels lead a relatively sedentary existence, with their major role being to continuously filter and "sample" their environment, which provides marine biologists with an essential tool for analysing water and environmental quality control. A decline in the mussel proliferation may indicate that the area has become over polluted and therefore, other sea life may not survive.

In Chinese medicine mussels have a strengthening effect on the liver and kidneys. This action helps to enhance the liver chi and improve the jing of the kidney and is therefore used to treat deficiencies of these areas such as impotence and lower back pain, as well as building the blood. Thermally they are a warming food with a salty flavour which is beneficial for those who crave sweet flavour.

Saffron Mussels

**Remember the old advise of not eating a mussel that has not opened during the cooking process.
It is preferable to discard any ones with closed shells.*

6 saffron threads
½ cup of warm water
1 kg mussels
1 tablespoon of extra virgin olive oil
½ Spanish onion, finely sliced
2 teaspoons of ginger, minced
2 cloves of garlic, chopped
1 cup of verjuice or mirin
½ cup of chopped spring onions
¼ cup of chopped coriander
1 lime, zest and juice
1 lemon, zest and juice
Cracked black pepper

- Place saffron threads in ½ cup of warm water to draw out their delicate flavour. Steep for 30 minutes, before using
- Clean mussels thoroughly by placing in a basin of cold water and then rub their shells together to eliminate any sand or other particles that may cling to the meat. Scrub the shells with steel wool, if desired. Remove and discard the 'beard' that hangs off to one side
- In a heavy base fry pan, heat the oil over a moderate heat and add onion, ginger and garlic. Sauté gently until the onion is transparent. Add mussels, saffron water and threads, wine or mirin
- Reduce heat to low, cover with a lid and simmer for about 5 minutes until the shells have opened. Add remaining ingredients and heat through well
- Season with black pepper and serve immediately

A Vine Romance

"In his day basil, the royal herb, was for keeping the bedroom free of flies; it had not yet encountered its soul-mate, the tomato"

Jane Grigson

As a member of the Solonacae clan, tomatoes were once thought to be poisonous like their more sinister relatives - the deadly nightshades (eggplant, potato, tobacco). It wasn't until the early 1800's that they gained popularity in America, having earlier been shunned by the Europeans. The New Orleans Creoles introduced them to the South to punctuate their local fare. Ironically, it was the English who gave ketchup to the world. Having set up the East India Trading Company, they were naturally privy to a vast array of spice from the Orient, which enhanced the British penchant for piquant chutneys, pickles and sauces.

"Who's gonna make the gravy now?
I bet it won't taste the same
Just add flour, salt, a little red wine and don't forget a dollop of
tomato sauce for sweetness and that extra tang."

Paul Kelly

Ketchup was also known as 'tomato soy' and is now prevalent on tables across the globe. In Indonesia and Malaysia it as common in warungs and hawker stalls as their native soy sauce. Thus by the end of the First World War, tomatoes were beginning to enjoy culinary respect universally.

Most of us envisage sun drenched Mediterranean vines bursting with ripe fruit that will in turn become the foundation for sauces and salads. Sadly, commercially grown tomatoes in this country seem to lack flavour and texture and I encourage everyone to sample a real, organically grown tomato - or better still, grow your own - and marvel at the voluptuousness of the flesh and sweetness of the flavour.

Medicinally to the Chinese, tomatoes represent a cooling thermal energy that helps to relieve heat conditions including dehydration, high blood pressure and chi stagnation. Despite being an acidic fruit, once digested tomatoes have an alkalising effect, especially on the blood. On the contrary however, like citrus and the other nightshades, tomatoes can decalcify the system, slowly removing calcium from bones and teeth and transporting it to unwanted parts of the body such as the joints. Therefore, those suffering from arthritis and other inflammatory conditions should avoid excessive tomato ingestion.

The healing properties of tomatoes lie within the antioxidant lycopeine, an active cartenoid that protects against the oxidants that lie close to the cell membranes. Lycopeine provides the colour red in tomatoes; pink in guava, grapefruit and watermelon; and the orange in apricots. Recent studies demonstrate that the influence of lycopeines in the diet - especially in men - has been strongly associated with a decreased risk of cancer of the gastrointestinal tract, prostate and of the upper digestive tract.

Lycopeine assists in the regulation of male hormone status and carcinogen metabolism, modulation of the immune system and enables new blood vessels to form as cancer invades cells. Lycopeine is thermodynamically stable, thus it can sustain heat. Cartenoids are lipophilic - that is to say they have an affinity with fat - and their healing properties are accentuated when mild thermal processing has enhanced them. The most beneficial recipes include gently cooked tomatoes that are then drizzled with olive oil thus enhancing the lipophilic properties of the cartenoid. Synthetic extracts of lycopeine are now available, however wouldn't it be so much more delicious to source and enjoy the natural alternative?

Skin Deep

Bioflavanoids

Also known as vitamin P because of their permeability factor, bioflavanoids improve the integrity of the cell membrane and facilitate the smooth passage of oxygen, carbon dioxide and other nutrients through the capillary walls. Therefore helping to prevent haemorrhage and rupture of capillaries and maybe used in the treatment of bleeding gums, bruising and weak capillaries.

Vitamin P works synergistically with vitamin C by enhancing its utilisation within the body and protecting against loss of vitamin C when it encounters oxygen. It is found in the pith and rind of citrus fruits; dark red fruit (think dark red, think good for the blood) such as cherries, grapes, blackcurrants and blackberries; as well as tomatoes, grapes, apricots and papaya. It is comprised of harmonious components including catechin and quercetin; flavones and flavanols -all powerful antioxidants.

A Time for Lime

Indigenous to South Eastern Asia, this warm climate fruit is most famous for keeping the British Navy alive on their voyages to the tropics in the eighteenth and nineteenth centuries. The rich vitamin C content of limes provided essential nutrients to ward off a devastating 'deficiency' disease known as Scurvy. Thus, the sailors were nicknamed "Limeys". Arabian traders brought limes to the Western world. Christopher Columbus transported them to the Americas on his second voyage in 1493.

Limes (citrus aurantifolia) are a small, sour, citrus fruit with a season that extends from March through to August, making them an appropriate remedial fruit to enjoy throughout the colder months. Smooth limes have a stronger skin than their zesty relatives and can survive the severity of hot tropical climes. However, they will not sustain frost and are quite fussy about thriving within a cooler climate.

Therapeutic Notes

Two main varieties Mexican and Tahitian are available in Australia. The Tahitian variety is the most popular of the small, shrub-like citrus trees, with its season peaking in autumn. The Kaffir or Makrut Lime, also known as the Wild Lime, is an essential ingredient of Thai cuisine. They will also grow in tropical parts of Australia. The minced leaves are used extensively in certain Javanese food and in Filipino dishes the chopped peel is made into a sweetmeat with milk and coconut. The pickled fruit, applied as a poultice, will allay neuralgia. Eaten, it is effective in relieving indigestion. It often accompanies spiced curries such as those featured in Indian cuisine to facilitate digestion.

This piquant fruit just might be the tropical traveller's saviour as its juice has the ability to dispel the irritation and swelling of mosquito bites, and may be taken as a tonic for the digestive system to relieve stomach ailments Limes have a cooling nature with an astringent flavour and antiseptic properties.

They are particularly beneficial to counteract diets high in saturated fats and protein by encouraging the formation of bile, which is essential for the catabolic process of food breakdown.
A squeeze of lime with hot water in the morning may facilitate a mild liver cleansing action for some, while others may find it helps to soothe convulsive coughs and headaches. Primitively, the leaves were used as a poultice for skin diseases and applied to the abdomen of new mothers after childbirth.

Limes are grown with fewer chemicals than lemons and they yield at least four times more citric acid content than oranges. Individuals with ailments such as excessive stomach acid or ulcers should not use them.

Limes are a useful remedy in the treatment of dysentery, colds, flu and parasite infestation due to their powerful antiseptic, antimicrobial and mucus-resolving actions. They can destroy putrefactive bacteria in both the intestine and mouth. Used to purify the breath, limes also cleanse the blood, help to lower hypertension, enhance blood circulation and strengthen the blood vessels.

Grapefruit

For most of my childhood I was brainwashed with the notion that ½ a glass of grapefruit juice every morning was good for you. My Dad would arise very early and partake in his "5BX 11-Minute-A-Day" exercise regime - much to the sheer horror of his children who could envisage nothing more inappropriate first thing in the morning. He'd follow this ritual with half glass of grapefruit juice with a hearty fry up of eggs, bacon and hot English mustard. This notion I'm sure was inspired by the 70s grapefruit diet. In short the citric acid from the juice would allegedly 'cut' the grease from the breakfast. However since both are acidic - the fry up being acid forming - seemed to negate the good intention.

Grapefruit as a whole food does have many positives. It is the pectin (not the juice) that forms the cell membrane the can help to lower LDLs and decrease the risk of heart disease, aid digestion and assist in alcohol detoxification.

The medicinal benefits of grapefruit seed extract are many. It maybe diluted with water to act as a bactericide and fungicide when washing salad vegetables and sterilising laundry - and is useful for travellers as it can added to filtered drinking water to kill unwanted parasites. If taken daily itwill help to prevent travellers' diarrhoea. The extract is also particularly beneficial in the treatment of Candida, drying damp and other fungus related conditions due to its ability to inhibit bacterial growth.

Being rich in vitamin C and bioflavanoids, grapefruits (named for the way the grow in grapelike clusters) also possess potassium, calcium, magnesium and lycopeine that is found in the pink variety. After oranges they are the second most grown fruit and their heritage traces to the West Indies. Citric acid is mildly astringent, an antioxidant and is used throughout the food industry.

The contraindications associated with excessive citrus intake is that it can interfere with calcium levels and too much may calcify the system, drawing calcium from teeth and bones. Those who enjoy a dairy free life might need to increase their intake of calcium rich foods such as dark green leafy vegetables, nuts and seeds and whole sardines.

It is also important to note that when using aluminium foil for baking, lemon is never added as the acid from the lemon combined with aluminium can become toxic.

Other citrus fruits may also yield abundant nutrient such as grapefruit (named for the way they grow in grape-like clusters). The pectin that forms the cell membrane of this fruit can help to lower LDL cholesterol levels and decrease the risk of heart disease, aid digestion and assist alcohol detoxification.

The abundance of vitamin C found in citrus fruits is well documented; yet, they also contain a lesser-known vital ingredient called bioflavonoids. Also known as vitamin P because of their permeability factor, bioflavonoids improve the integrity of the cell membrane, and facilitate the smooth passage of oxygen, carbon dioxide and other nutrients through the capillary walls. Thus they may help to prevent a possible haemorrhage or a rupture of capillaries, and they are especially helpful in the treatment of bleeding gums or any condition with bruised or weak capillaries.

Vitamin P works synergistically with vitamin C by enhancing its utilisation within the body and protecting against loss of vitamin C when it encounters oxygen. It is found in the pith and rind of citrus fruits. Dark red fruits such as cherries, grapes, blackcurrants and blackberries all contain rich bioflavonoids, as do apricots, papaya and tomatoes. The bioflavanoid activity lays in the skin of fruits and generally the darker the fruit the better. It is comprised of harmonious components including catechin and quercetin, flavones and flavonols - powerful antioxidants.

Berries and Cherries

Everybody loves cherries, especially little girls who love to dress up and adorn their ears with a pair of fresh cherry earrings. Where tomatoes aggravate inflammation, cherries are known to remedy arthritis and gout and help to alleviate rheumatism. They are detoxifying and have anti-putrefying properties, which help to process stagnant animal proteins and aid the colon to enhance bowel motility. The bioflavanoid activity is in the skin of both fruits and generally the darker the fruit the better.

The natural sugar found in cherries do not transform to insulin, making them a safe fruit for diabetes patients. Their potassium level is very high, so to is vitamin C and bioflavanoids. As with all foods, the high nutrient contents can only be beneficial when the fresh, unadulterated product is consumed.

Berries including "strawberry, raspberry, blackberry, blueberry, huckleberry, mulberries and pomegranate and grapes) contain the phytonutrients ellagic acid and resveratrol, known to regenerate liver cells. Grapes additionally are a source of the substantial antioxidant proanthocyanidin, which can protect liver and other cells" in the body according to my most recent teacher Paul Pitchford, author of Healing with Whole Foods.

Dedicated Coconut

The Grinning Face

Back in the old days this tropical fruit was known as cocoanut, a term derived from 16th century Portuguese and Spanish cocos, meaning, "grinning face" - because of the three small holes on its coconut shell.

Approximately one third of the world's population depends on the humble coconut with one billion coconut palms blowing throughout the tropics, which in turn produce over 50 billion coconuts per annum - mostly for consumption as detailed below – but also dried as copra – a valued trade commodity used in the production of soap and also for lighting in the 19th century.

Here's a look at the how and why of the life of a coconut - which refers to the entire coconut palm, the seed, or the fruit - but is not a botanical nut.

1. Coconut water – this is the clear to lightly cloudy sweet nectar of a young coconut. Do not waste your time or money with the commercial processed junk food on the market. DIY with a cleaver or a screwdriver and a hammer. The water is highly refreshing and rehydrating and maybe processed to make alcohol

2. Coconut meat – this is the meat (endosperm) or flesh of the young coconut is softer and more gelatinous than that in a mature coconut and you can scrape out with a spoon to eat straight away or process with the water and a probiotic to make coconut yoghurt – see recipe

3. Coconut milk – is made from the flesh of fresh coconuts with coconut water, then straining it to remove some of the fat. According to my dear friend Bali Janet of the famed Casa Luna Restaurant and Cooking School, is far superior to the supermarket variety, which of course can be used if you have no time to make the real thing. The Balinese only use coconut milk and never the 'cream'

4. Coconut cream – has a thicker consistency, more like a paste and is made with a higher ratio of coconut to water. It is typically used to thicken and flavour Thai red and green curries.

You will notice the cream when you open a can of coconut milk as it separates leaving a thick yogurt-like substance on top – cream - and a thinner liquid remaining below - milk. Obviously, the coconut cream has more fat and this is why some rich Thai recipes call for it as it helps to release the fats in order to fry off the aromatic curry pastes so they provide a richer more luxurious flavour

5. Shredded or desiccated coconut - not to be confused with desecrated as I read in one recipe recently! This is the made from shredded dried coconut. Desiccated means to remove the moisture from it thus preserving it.

6. Coconut oil - extracted from the kernel or meat of matured coconuts harvested from the coconut palm. Ensure you buy certified organic coconut oil as conventional products may have added solvents such as hexane, which is used to extract cooking oils from seeds.

Prior to World War II Asian military occupation of the Philippines and other South Pacific islands resulted on the once-plentiful supply of coconut oil was effectively cut off from the United States. As the post war industrial revolution kicked in, manufacturers began to develop alternative sources of cooking oils – hence the "You ought to be congratulated" phase of mono and polyunsaturated fat boom gave rise to a very profitable promotion of vegetable oils.

To quote Dr. Mercola, a leading - albeit outspoken - expert on all things healthy "By the end of the 1950's, public opinion had turned totally against saturated fats like butter (and coconut oil). Saturated fats were blamed for raising cholesterol and cholesterol was now viewed as the evil enemy, the culprit responsible for the steep rise in heart disease."

We said bye-bye to butter, eggs and coconut oil and hello to allegedly heart healthy vegetable fats and the dreaded and deadly processed soy bean boom, determined to see the sinking of tropical oils harvested in poorer countries who may not have been able to defend their livelihood.

See also You can't milk a soy bean.

The Tree of Life

In 2004 the Coconut Research Centre declared the medium chain fatty acids (MCFA) that are found in coconut to "help to lower the risk of both atherosclerosis and heart disease. It is primarily due to the MCFA in coconut oil that makes it so special and so beneficial." (Source: Coconut Research Centre)

In addition, these medium chin fatty acids aka Medium Chain Triglycerides (MCTs) stimulate thermogenesis - the process where your body produces heat by increased burning of fat - this is a good thing for people who are trying to lose body fat.

According to the American Journal of Clinical Nutrition, (Vol. 87, No. 3, 621-626, March 2008), "Clinical studies have shown that consumption of MCTs leads to greater energy expenditure than does consumption of long-chain triacylglycerols. Such studies suggest that MCT consumption may be useful for weight management".

Coconut Yoghurt

I rarely eat dairy so I am forever devising concoctions that are dairy free for my clients who are dreaming of that cheesy feeling. With no cow or sheep's milk yoghurt for breakfast, necessity and consumer demand led to my first trial batch of coconut yoghurt. Here's how I made it…

2 young Thai coconuts,
   opened and flesh removed to yield about 1½ cups of flesh
1¼ cups coconut water from the 2 coconuts you will open,
   so strain well
1 teaspoon probiotic powder
   (I used 4 capsules of Metagenics Ultra Flora DF)

- In a Thermomix – or other fancy high speed blender – puree the coconut meat and water until it is thick and creamy
- Stir in the probiotic and then transfer into a sterilised jar, seal and incubate in a dehydrator at 100 C for 4-6 hours
- Remove from dehydrator, allow to cool and then chill
- Use within 5 days

*Yields about 500 ml or more depending on how much flesh you get from your coconuts

Incas, Aztecs, Mayans and Mexicans

Sounds like bad cab ride eh? Well the fact is that these dudes have coughed up some of the most superlicious ancient ingredients known to modern man. As a rule I adopt a SLOWER principle. That is Seasonal, Local, Organic, Wholefoods, Environmental and Regional so I use imported products sparingly, however most of the celebrated superfoods are imported.

Here's a select few – just enough to survive the foodie fashion fad!

Acai Brazil
Acai is an energizing berry from the Amazon. A little like macqui in that it contains high levels of polyphenols and anthocyanins, which helps to detoxify and cleanse the blood.

AFA Blue Green Algae Oregon, USA
E3Live® is my number one supplemental superfood. It's a raw fresh water algae, known as Aphanizomenon flos-aquae (AFA). It is very special because it is wild-harvested from only one place on earth, Upper Klamath Lake in Oregon, USA.
I love it because it provides over 64 easily absorbed vitamins, minerals, micronutrients and enzymes and helps alkalize the body, as it is a complete, raw, living food. It also has naturally occurring green, blue and magenta pigments that reflect the presence of fresh chlorophyll and an anti-inflammatory compound called phycocyanin. I buy it here

Agave South Africa and Mexico
Agave is a commercially produced nectar from in South Africa and Mexico. Sweeter than honey, though less viscous and comes in light and dark forms. You'll recognize the cactus it comes from when you see it. It's that big flower like plant that you just wanna hug but know you can't 'cos it's spiky!
Agave syrup stores its energy as inulin, also known as fructans or levulose and is beneficial because it feeds the probiotic bacteria in our digestive system.

This is absorbed slowly into the bloodstream giving it a low glycaemic index so it is suitable for most diabetics.

Cacao – raw ancient superfood
Recent controversy surrounds raw cacao at the time of writing this and I've asked the experts including Sarah Wheeler a raw chocolatier who makes PureMelt Chocolate.
We both agree that raw cacao is indeed a superfood, one that nourishes, nurtures and energises. Raw cacao is a bitter food that is essential for liver clearance.
Cacao's selling point is that it is nutrient dense with antioxidants to help support the immune system and magnesium that is a relaxant. It is a stimulant however and will certainly give you energy, a bit like caffeine, so go easy at the end of the day with it.

Camu camu - Peru
Camu Camu (Mycaria Dubia) is a bushy tree that grows in the rivers of the Amazon. The yellow fruit is prized for its immune boosting properties including the relief of herpes (always welcome!), blisters and other viral infections. They reckon it's an energy tonic that promotes good heart health and circulation.

Cats claw – Peru
Cats Claw (Uncaria tomentosa) is another Amazonian immune tonic that also allegedly supports digestion too. It contains immuno-stimulant and anti-inflammatory properties of that may help the body fight off viral and respiratory infections and protect against degenerative diseases.

Chia seeds – Colombia
Chia belongs to the mint family and dates back to pre-Colombian Aztec times.
It is used as a natural thickening agent because it swells and becomes mucilaginous or slippery when liquid is added. This makes it a great tonic to repair the mucous membranes of the intestinal wall that may be depleted due to ulceration and inflammation. It's more than a complete protein as it contains nine amino acids.

RECIPES AND REMEDIES FROM AUSTRALIA'S LEADING SPA CHEF

Choc Chia Muffins

1 ½ cup spelt flour
1 ½ teaspoons bicarbonate soda
1 cup hazelnuts finely processed or 1 ½ cup hazelnut meal
1 ½ teaspoon vanilla powder
4 tablespoons coconut sugar
½ cup ground cacao nibs
1 ½ cup dates finely processed
3 tablespoons chia seeds soaked in ½ cup water for ten
   minutes
½ cup coconut oil, melted
1 cup almond milk
extra coconut oil, melted for greasing

- Preheat oven to 170 C. Brush a 24 hole muffin tray with
  coconut oil
- Combine dry ingredients and mix thoroughly
- Add soaked chia seeds, coconut oil and almond milk
  gradually
- Spoon mixture in muffin tray and bake for approximately
  45 minutes

Lucuma - Peru

Lucuma is a sub-tropical Peruvian fruit known as the "Gold of the Incas" which is celebrated for its colour that contains the immune boosting anti-oxidant beta-carotene. Sold in raw powder form it is used as a natural sweetener and popular as an ice cream flavour.

Maca - Incas

Maca is a hormone regulator or an adaptogen, which means that it may balance the entire endocrine system. It contains unique alkaloids that promote the optimal functioning of the hypothalamus and pituitary master glands, which may in turn balance the levels of estrogen, progesterone and testosterone that are produced. If these hormones are regulated the function of the ovaries and adrenal glands may also be enhanced.

This is why it is used to relive symptoms of menopause including hot flushes, vaginal dryness and depression. Maca is used as a fertility enhancer for both men and women and is also used to increase energy, stamina, enhance libido and treat impotence. Up ya go!

Maqui – Chile
Macqui is a deep purple berry from the south of Chile and has anti-inflammatory benefits. As it is a berry that lovely sweet taste and contains high levels of polyphenols and anthocyanins that helps to detoxify and cleanse the blood.

Mesquite – Mexico
I love mesquite! It is actually flour made from a leguminous pod that is native to northern Mexico. It has a rich, sweet and creamy taste - a lot like caramel - and gives smoothies and raw treats an added depth of flavour, especially when blended with raw cacao for a delicious treat.
It has a low GI of 25 because of its dense mineral content that helps to stabilize blood sugar levels. High in protein and contains significant quantities of calcium, magnesium, potassium, iron and zinc, it is also rich in the amino acid lysine.

Yacon – Peru
Yacom is a Peruvian tuber (root vegetable) that grows in the low valleys of the Andes. It possesses a sweet taste with a slightly crunchy texture a bit like watermelon or jicama. It boasts pre-biotic activity in the body, which means that it encourages the proliferation of good bacteria in the gut and enhances digestive function and elimination.

Gowings peppermint superfoods Paleo slice
Image ©Brrad Wagner

Paleo Power

I'm becoming more and more intrigued by the Paleo way of life. The more I read, the more it makes sense, especially from an unprocessed, wholefoods point of view. Essentially it's about minimising your grain intake and upping the ante on premium organic meat and enjoying an abundance of sustainable fish. Most importantly it is all about hunter-gatherer, so masses of great vegetables are a must.

Therefore I've been experimenting with snacks to eat while on this pathway and I've come up with a ripsnorter of a treat! It needs refrigerating in the warmer weather, which we're loving here in Byron this summer. Substitute the nuts, dried fruit and seeds for whatever you have in your pantry and just use more vanilla or maybe lemon essence or zest if you have no peppermint oil.

Gowings Peppermint Paleo Slice

This is the ultimate raw Paleo treat – no cooking required.

- ¾ cup currants
- ¾ cup dried apricots
- ¾ cup hazelnuts
- ¾ cup Brazil nuts
- ¾ cup sunflower seeds – activated if possible
- ¾ cup cacao
- ¾ cup shredded coconut
- 2 teaspoons vanilla
- 3 drops peppermint oil (food grade)
- 2 teaspoons agave syrup
- ¾ cup coconut oil, melted – plus a little extra for greasing

- Line a rectangular or square cake tin with baking paper. Brush with coconut oil In a food processor, blitz currants, apricots nut and seeds until they resemble coarse breadcrumbs
- Add cacao, ½ cup shredded coconut, vanilla, peppermint and agave
- Fold through melted coconut oil Press into the lined tin, scatter extra shredded coconut and goji berries on top
- Refrigerate for at least 4 hours to allow to set
- Turn out onto a board when hard and cut into squares
Keep chilled and use within 7 days

Amazeballs Deluxe

These luxurious superfood balls will have you zinging all the way to Christmas Day - or any other festive day - with bells on. Start out with the nuts, some dried fruit and then add a selection of your favourite superfoods such as mesquite, macqui or maca.

1 cup almonds
1 cup macadamia nuts
½ cup currants
½ cup Medjool dates
2 tablespoons raw cacao
2 tablespoons cacao butter, melted – I use this brand
½ cup coconut oil, melted
1 teaspoon mesquite powder
1 teaspoon cinnamon
1 teaspoon organic vanilla essence
Coconut for rolling

- Place all ingredients in a high speed food processor and blitz together until the mixture starts to combine and stick
- Roll into golf ball sized balls, roll in coconut and refrigerate for at least 2 hours before serving
- This balls are best kept chilled and do not like being out of the fridge for more than an hour

Paleo Breakfast Superfood Smoothie

I can't take all the credit for this little ripper 'cos my super smooth chef Jasmine (a.k.a. Jazzy Pops) did all the work, but she insisted I call it this so here it is. We have one of these most mornings to break the <u>Paleo Intermittent Fasting</u> 16 hour fast. It's packed full of everything a chef could need for a long hot stint in the kitchen.

1 handful organic kale, washed and dried
½ cup assorted berries of your choice
1 coconut – water only, save the flesh for making <u>coconut yoghurt</u>
2 teaspoons ground chia seeds
1 teaspoon mesquite
1 teaspoon maca powder
1 tablespoon protein powder – we use a local called Ezy Protein Powder available here
1 teaspoon cacao

- Place all ingredients in a blender and puree until completely smooth
- Add a little ice if desired

Grace and Gratitude

This literary journey started life in 1999 and has had more than a few hiatuses on the back burner. Now she's cooked, ready to carve and serve.

I am so deeply grateful for the following people who dress the table of my life.

My beloved bestie, Nigel Carboon who subliminally steered this project to the book drive in. Without him, it would still be a pile of words, whispers and unpublished wisdom. I love him unconditionally and every girl needs a Noo Noo like mine. He brings my food to life with his photos, tears to my eyes, laughter to my lungs and love to my heart. Thanks Noo.

For my darling man Lance Innes. Although our journey has just begun, it is as though we have always been one. I am deeply grateful for the love you have poured into preparing The Healing Feeling for print. May the words on these pages continue to resonate with your being and invigorate your heart.

To Russell 'Ruski' Price who edited the book in between geological stints in Africa. A strappingly handsome fellow and follower of Chinese Wise Whispers who can whisk words into a stir-fry and stroke your funny bone while he's at it.

Thanks to Flip Shelton for finding the time to write such an entertaining foreword all the way from Rio de Janeiro amongst a global relocation, months of dislocation and culture shock.

To my Cosmic Sister 'Bali' Janet DeNeefe for her encouragement, direction, adventures, food, music, love and laughter.

My boundless gratitude extends to Claire 'Sugar' O'Connell. A woman who lights up every room. She is a gourmet goddess of style baked with dynamically visual and compelling award-winning graphic design.

Byron blessings to Becca "The beautiful Los Angelean Letterer" Clason who agreed to scribe the cover in such a short timeline - oh how I love her work! Becca is a letterer and graphic designer based in California who loves crafting letters with pen on paper.

To Lyndy "Tricky" Lee for being such an amazing two-tone human being, a passionate cook and a kaleidoscopic Byron entity.

Over the last thirty years, I may have broken bread, mentored, learned, loved and laughed whole-heartedly with this crew. Often. The following folk have supported and endorsed my work worldwide.

Al Kennedy, the Bay Seafood Market, the Blake Family, Brett Kingman, Brookfarm, Brook Ramage, Chris Gowing, Duncan & Debo McNab, Filomena Perra, George Michael, German Dimaano, the Green Grocer, Healthtalks TV, Helen Wood, Jasmine Norton, Jenny & Steve Carboon, Jill Kelly, Johnny & Mafi Watson, Jeannie Stephen, Jemma Gawned, Jude Nicholls, Kay O'Sulluvan, Ketut Suardana, Kylie Mitchell-Smith, Lane Badger, Le Cordon Bleu, Linda Bull, Lyndy Lee, Max Blake, Matt Preston, Megan Dalla-Camina, Michael Cook, Michael Gow, Mondo Organics, Natalie Kringoudis, Nelly le Comte, Nic Carram, Nikki Fisher, OneSixOne, Pamela Bakes, Paul Pitchford, Randolph Gowing, Remy Tancred, Rita Erlich, Roberto Scheriani, Russell Price, Russell White, Sally Browne, Sally Macindoe, Sandra Uijland, Shannon Bennett, Sionach Waugh, SWB, Victoria Cosford - and finally to my dear, dear friend Vika Bull. Thank you.

Whole Happiness

If you are reading this then you will have a real, three dimensional page turning version of *The Healing Feeling* in your hot little hands! I self published the first edition as an ebook, however the demand has been so great that a print run was needed. This coincides with a new initiative I have birthed and trademarked called Whole Happiness™.

Along my journey with the healing arts I have observed a deeper desire by the guests, clients and patients I have met for something greater than spa and wellness. The pursuit of happiness is fundamental to our consciousness and I am of the opinion that a holistic and all encompassing approach to happiness is one of the keys.

Therefore, I am thrilled to officially launch my new project, Whole Happiness™, an evolution of *The Healing Feeling*. This is a powerful initiative driven by a conscious awareness that happiness is a multi-faceted state of being. The need to thrive is beyond raw food, yoga moves and green smoothies. It is about finding our true self, our essential nature, and allowing all of these aspects to integrate into ourselves.

Abundance, wellness, wealth, joy and the spiritual pursuit of inner peace are key emotional and physical drivers contributing to the Whole Happiness™ state. Above and beyond, it is our innate human desire to express an attitude of gratitude that brings the ultimate state of Whole Happiness™.

Incentives include our Whole Happiness™ publishing service that helps others realise their publishing dreams - whether it be online or in print - and life changing keynote conference presentations that deliver the Whole Happiness™ menu to the ever-expanding wellness industry and the worldwide sustainable sector.

So thank you for reading my book and I sincerely hope that you have enjoyed the flavour of *The Healing Feeling*. I trust that it has made you lick your lips and lift the corners of your mouth!

Samantha Gowing
Byron Bay, September 2013

Samantha Gowing

Samantha is a product of the Seventies, born in the Sixties, and has been working with food since the Eighties. In the Nineties she became the licensee of the historic Grace Darling Hotel, in the Australian football heartland of Collingwood, steering it to multi awarding-winning victory - including a coveted chef's hat - for eight years.

A passionate entrepreneur, she founded her globally recognized business Gowings Food Health Wealth in 2000. This provides culinary and marketing solutions to the wellness industry. Sam transplanted herself from the gritty inner Melbourne suburb of Collingwood to lush Byron Bay in 2008 to further her holistic study, research, and to surf the pristine waters of the north coast.

Sam holds a Diploma of Health Science, Nutrition and is a member of the Australian Traditional Medicine Society. She has certified with Paul Pitchford, author of Healing with Whole Foods and has recently completed a Graduate Certificate as part of her pursuit of the world class Le Cordon Bleu Master of Gastronomic Tourism degree.

When she is not in the kitchen or the ocean, she mentors likeminded whippersnappers who have a yearning for all things well and healthy in business.

Index

Acai 129

Aduki beans 42, 43, 44, 89, 90, 97

AFA Blue Green Algae 129

Agave 23, 129, 133

Almond milk 76, 131

Almonds 21, 23, 49, 56, 76, 99, 101, 134

Amaranth 72, 73, 81

Apple 56, 69, 76, 86

Apricot 56, 61, 91, 119, 120, 124, 133

Artichokes 48

Asparagus 56

Avocado 56

Balsamic vinegar 99

Banana 56

Barley 56, 58, 59, 68, 73, 74, 87

Beans 56, 77, 89, 96, 97

Beef 40, 58, 93, 116

Beets 41, 47, 48, 56, 70, 71, 74

Berries 31, 98, 99, 124, 135

Black beans 40, 97

Black-eyed peas 95

Blackberries 120, 124

Blackcurrant 120, 124

Blueberry 65, 124

Brazil nuts 56, 133

Broad beans 93, 96, 97

Broccoli 56

Brussels sprouts 32, 56

Buckwheat 74, 75, 76

Butter 22, 23, 24, 56, 78, 126, 127

Cabbage 56

Cacao 24, 25, 130, 131, 132, 133, 134, 135

Cacao butter 134

Calendula flowers 46

Camu camu 130

Cardamom 86

Carrots 26, 41, 56

Cashew 23, 24, 56

Cashew milk 24

Cats claw 130

Cauliflower 56

Cayenne 51, 109

Celery 56, 101

Cherries 99, 120, 124

Chestnuts 42, 43

Chia seeds 130, 131, 135

Chicken 40, 59, 79, 100

Chickpeas 40, 89, 95, 97

Chili 26, 106, 109, 112

Chives 47, 106, 110

Cider vinegar 23, 32, 49

Cinnamon 86, 134

Cleavers 46

Coconut 24, 76, 86, 121, 125, 126, 127, 128, 133, 134, 135

Coconut cream 24, 44, 126

Coconut milk 126

Coconut oil 22, 23, 24, 44, 53, 78, 86, 126, 127, 131, 133, 134

Coconut sugar 131

Coconut water 126, 128

Coconut yoghurt 127, 128, 135

Coriander 43, 44, 91, 113, 117

Corn 76, 77, 79, 85

Cucumber 32, 41, 56

Cumin 44, 51, 91, 113

Currants 83, 133, 134

Dairy 22, 54, 100, 122, 123, 128

Dates 23, 24, 86, 131, 134

Dulse flakes 51

Echinacea 46

Edamame 40

EFA (Essential Fatty Acids) 41

Egg 26, 56, 59, 78, 127

Eggplant 56, 59, 118

Fava beans 40, 93, 94

Figs 51, 52, 53, 127

Fish 35, 40, 41, 56, 100, 113, 133

Garlic 48, 51, 92, 106, 107, 108, 109, 112, 113, 116, 117

Ginger 21, 42, 43, 48, 59, 60, 71, 80, 86, 92, 101, 106, 111, 112, 113, 117

Grape 120, 124

Grapefruit 56, 119, 122, 123

Green chilies 44, 48, 113

Green peas 49, 97

Green peppers 56

Greens 56

Haricot beans 94

Hazelnut 131, 133

Hazelnuts 56, 131, 133

Honey 24, 47, 48, 59, 64, 65, 76, 86, 129

Huckleberry 124

Kaffir lime 92, 121

Kale 56, 135

Kelp 57, 21

Koji 58

Kuzu 60, 61

Lecithin 41, 76

Leeks 106, 110

Lemon 23, 43, 47, 48, 51, 53, 60, 83, 112, 117, 123, 133

Lentils 40, 89, 94, 96, 97, 100

Lettuce 26, 56

Lima beans 40, 42, 94

Lime 21, 32, 49, 77, 86, 99, 101, 113, 117, 120, 121

Lime leaves 47, 92

Lime olive oil 101

Linseeds 49, 56

Lucuma 131

Maca 131, 132, 134, 135

Macadamia nuts 134

Macadamia oil 21, 32, 56, 41, 99, 113

Mango 56, 99

Maqui 132

Mesquite 132, 134, 135

Milk 64, 67, 73, 78, 98, 100

Millet 56, 73, 79, 80

Mint 26, 47, 49, 83, 92, 130

Mirin 21, 59, 101, 117

Miso 21, 30, 58, 59

Mulberries 124

Mung beans 41, 90, 91, 92, 96

Mussels 116, 117

Mustard 32, 43, 122

Mustard cress 49, 56

Mustard seeds 44

Nectarine 56, 99

Nori 21, 57

Oats 41, 56, 68, 80, 81, 100, 116

Okra 56

Olive oil 47, 49, 56, 83, 101, 113, 117, 119

Onion 44, 48, 56, 101, 106, 108, 109, 110, 116, 117

Orange 56, 78, 109, 121, 122, 123

Paleo 133, 135

Papaya 56, 67, 120, 124

Parnship 56

Parsley 32, 47, 56

Peach 56

Peanuts 100

Pear 52, 53, 156

Peas 49, 56

Pecan nuts 41, 56, 99

Pepitas 32, 47, 86, 101

Pepper (spice) 32, 47, 49, 83, 99, 109, 117

Peppercorn 92

Peppermint oil 133

Pine nuts 83

Pineapple 56, 67

Plum vinegar 21

Polenta 76, 77, 78

Pomegranate 47, 124

Pork 40

Potatoes 31, 56, 118

Prawns 26

Probiotics 64

Protein powder 135

Prunes 32

Pumpkin 31, 42, 44, 56, 58, 59, 100

Pumpkin seeds 100, 101

Quinoa 42, 49, 50, 56, 72, 79, 81, 82, 83

Radishes 56, 99

Ramen noodles 59

Raspberry 22, 23, 65, 99, 124

Raspberry vinegar 99

Red kidney beans 93, 97

Rhubarb 52, 53, 74

Rice 50, 56, 58, 59, 72, 79, 84, 85, 86, 87, 93, 101

Rice paper 26, 53

Rocket 101

Rosewater 22, 23, 47, 86

Rye 56, 68, 80, 87, 88

Saffron 117

Salt 23, 24, 51, 78, 83, 113

Sardines 41, 83, 122, 123

Seaweed 21, 44, 57

Sesame 43, 50, 51, 56, 59, 100

Sesame oil 59, 113

Shallot 32, 92, 106, 109, 110

Shiitake mushrooms 42, 59, 62, 63

Shoyu 60, 74

Soy grits 76

Soy sauce 118

Soybeans 40, 58, 95, 127

Spelt 131

Spinach 44, 56, 59, 70, 74, 81

Spring onions 43, 110, 113, 117

Sprouts 32, 47, 48, 49, 70, 72, 91, 98, 99, 101

Squash 56

Strawberry 124

Sunflower seeds 51, 86, 133

Tahini 51

Tamari 21, 30, 43, 51, 113

Tofu 59, 92, 101

Tomato 56, 116, 118, 119, 120, 124

Tomato paste 44

Turkey 40, 41, 73, 98, 99, 100

Turmeric 86, 111, 113, 114

Turnip 56

Umeboshi 21, 60, 61

Vanilla 131, 133, 134

Verjuice 117

Vermicelli noodles 26

Wheat 58, 68, 69, 70, 73, 85, 87

Wheatgrass 41, 69, 70, 71

Yacon 132

Yoghurt 64, 65, 86

Zucchini 56

Recipe index

Salad of sea vegetables with kelp noodles, 21

Individual raw-spberry rose cakes, 23

Raw tiramisu: Coconut, cashews and dates in disguise, 24

Rice paper rolls with prawns and omelette, 26

Raw Brussels sprouts slaw, 32

Wontons of roasted chestnut, ginger and aduki beans, 43

Aduki, pumpkin & coconut curry, 44

Lymphatic Tisane, 46

Beetroot, pomegranate & rosewater salad, 47

Zenergising Beet Top Tea, 48

Salad of shoots, nuts, peas and leaves with red quinoa, 49

Gomasio, 51

Sunny sunflower whip, 51

Autumn rolls of fig and rhubarb with rhubarb puree, 53

Ume-sho-kuzu, 60

Yoghurt recipe, 65

Wheatgrass Beetini, 71

Buckwheat with coconut and almonds, 76

Citrus polenta pancakes, 78

Sardine fillets with minted quinoa, currant and pine nut salad, 83

Mahatma Breakfast, 86

Forever Mung - Minted mung beans with ginger, 92

Salad of turkey, berries, nuts with local sprouts, micro herbs, 99

Seared lime tofu with crunchy shoots, nuts & leaves, 101

A gingerly paste for winter, 113

Whole fish with tamari and ginger, 113

Saffron mussels, 117

Coconut yoghurt with fresh figs, 127

Coconut yoghurt, 128

Choc chia muffins, 131

Gowings peppermint paleo slice, 133

Amazeballs Deluxe, 134

Paleo breakfast superfood smoothie, 135

Printed in Great Britain
by Amazon